THE PERFECT
KITTEN

THE PERFECT
KITTEN

PETER NEVILLE &
CLAIRE BESSANT

SPECIAL PHOTOGRAPHY BY JANE BURTON

HAMLYN

The Perfect Kitten
Peter Neville and Claire Bessant

First published in 1997 by
Hamlyn
an imprint of Reed Books Ltd
Michelin House, 81 Fulham Road, London SW3 6RB
and Auckland, Melbourne, Singapore and Toronto

Publishing Director: Laura Bamford

Executive Editor: Simon Tuite
Project Editor: Katie Cowan
Editor: Jane Royston

Art Director: Keith Martin
Executive Art Editor: Mark Stevens
Designer: Ginny Zeal
Illustrator: Jackie Harland
Picture Researcher: Wendy Gay
Photographer: Jane Burton

Production: Jo Allum and Dawn Mitchell

British Library Cataloguing-in-Publication Data
A catalogue record for this book is available from the British Library

ISBN 0 600 59152 2

Typeset in Goudy and $9^1/_2$ on 11pt Bookman Light

Produced by Mandarin Book Production
Printed and bound in China

CONTENTS

INTRODUCTION

Kittens are wonderful creatures. Tiny and vulnerable, yet already equipped with the innate skills and strength of design befitting a top-of-the-food-chain predator, a new kitten will occupy hours of your time but leave you all the richer for it. That beauty of feline athletic power and grace is legendary, but the cat's adaptability in so many varied environments and social circumstances has also made it arguably the most successful predatory mammal yet to evolve on earth. Make no mistake, as a species the cat moved in on us – not the other way around – over 4000 years ago for its own advantage, and each and every pet cat still only remains with us for all those things that it enjoys – warmth, company, shelter and food. Having said this, however, it is also true to say that if a cat expects a great deal it also gives an enormous amount in return, as you will discover from the day your kitten first arrives in your home.

From that day onwards, you will be a parent figure to your cat and, although it will grow up to be independent of mind and unique in personality, the first days and weeks are when it will need you most to help it to adapt to living in your human den. You will need to provide the best opportunity possible for your kitten to learn your ways and a few house rules, as well as how to enjoy your love, care and protection. At the same time you must also be willing to learn, as this is the time when your kitten will be teaching you how to respond to its every request – and most young kittens are remarkably successful at producing well-trained owners!

Vets and pet therapists agree that the vast majority of medical and behavioural problems arising in cats could be prevented by owners choosing cats which are suitable for them, by understanding them and looking after them properly, and by responding early to signs of distress. This book is intended to help you to see life from your kitten's point of view – how it perceives and relates to you, your other pets and your home. By understanding these things more clearly you will be able to care for your kitten in the best way possible, and you will know what to do and whom to turn to for advice if you are concerned in any way about its welfare.

As well as giving detailed advice on the practical aspects of caring for your kitten, from feeding to basic training and health care, part of the aim of this book is to address a growing concern of feline behaviourists about the way more and more cats are now being kept in urban environments. Behavioural problems in cats increasingly arise from the restricted lifestyle that many owners impose on them, and from a lack of understanding of their needs. While there is no shortage of love, or of concern when things go wrong, many people fail to realize just how specialized their pet cats are as predators, and that they need more than love to lead a happy life. Every cat requires mental stimulation and the opportunity at least to practise what it is, and what has shaped its every sense, bone, muscle and whisker – and that is to be a hunter, even if only of moving toys.

Your pet kitten is not just an appealing bundle of fur but a highly sensitive and emotional creature which will all too easily be upset or even made ill, and certainly made dull, by a lonely, unstimulating lifestyle as a pet kept in a city apartment if you do not understand and fulfil its needs – social, environmental and predatory. Subjugate its needs to yours and it will suffer; fulfil them and you will have the joy of sharing a friendship, and of appreciating to the full one of nature's finest products. From kitten to cat, the responsibility and the enjoyment are yours, and we hope that this book helps you to take enormous pleasure in both.

Acknowledgements

We would like to thank Sarah Whitehead for her enormous help in the research and preparation of this book, and Jane Burton, both for her stunning photography and for raising and organizing her kitten models so beautifully.

Simon Tuite and Katie Cowan at Hamlyn deserve much more than the customary authors' thanks for their editorial skills and encouragement. Their consideration and understanding throughout this production have gone well beyond the call of duty, and we are extremely grateful.

Special thanks also go to Gwen Bailey for writing the sister volume to this book, *The Perfect Puppy*, so well and so successfully that *The Perfect Kitten* was called for. We would also like to acknowledge the remarkable insights into feline and canine behaviour of Peter's colleagues at the Centre of Applied Pet Ethology (COAPE: PO Box 18, Tisbury, Wiltshire SP3 6LZ), especially Robin Walker MRCVS, and the late and sadly missed John Fisher.

Finally, our thanks to all our cats past and present, especially to the calm, collected Bullet, a London feral kitten who turned into the world's best country cat – may your hunting grounds be forever full and your place by the hearth ever warm!

Chapter One

THE RAW MATERIAL

Some people have owned cats all their lives – childhood memories are punctuated by cats of character, and they feel that home is incomplete without a resident feline. To others owning a cat is a pleasure discovered later in life, perhaps because they are unable to keep a dog or simply because they have become late converts to ailurophilia (the love of cats). Ironically, it is often those people who profess not to like cats who are 'adopted' by a stray cat or kitten, and who subsequently become the most ardent of cat enthusiasts.

In the UK, USA and most of the Western world, more cats than dogs are now kept as pets, taking over the latter's role of man's best friend. All around the globe cats have adapted incredibly well to a variety of environments and lifestyles, surviving and even thriving in extremes of temperature and harsh conditions, while as domesticated animals they have managed to combine their independent nature with an ability to share affection and live happily within our homes.

The pleasure of getting to know a new kitten – playing with it, feeding and training it, and watching it grow and develop – can be shared by all members of the family.

Whenever you enter the world of cat companionship (most people feel that they are 'owned' by their cats rather than the other way around, and would hesitate to label such free spirits as possessions), you should bear in mind that the kitten you choose is likely to spend at least 14 years with you – possibly even more. This makes choosing the right type of kitten for you and your family a vital first step, which will need to be given careful thought. The following information should help you to make some key decisions.

PEDIGREE OR NOT?

Mention that you have a cat and most people will envisage a non-pedigree individual – in fact, only about 10 per cent of all cats kept as pets are pedigree (pure-bred) animals. In general, even though many people are easily able to name a wide variety of dog breeds, they remain unaware of the extensive range of cat breeds that is now available.

Cats are naturally independent creatures, and are a delight to watch – both indoors and out – as they explore and learn about their environment.

There are probably several reasons for this, the first being that cats are very personal pets – they are not taken out for walks, or for trips in the car like dogs, so we may not even see very many breeds unless they belong to family or friends; indeed, some cat breeds have only recently been discovered or developed. Even when we come across new breeds we may not notice the more subtle differences between them, as most are roughly the same size and have the same general shape. In this, cats are also unlike their canine cousins, which vary from being smaller than a cat to the size of some ponies, as we cannot fail to notice!

Perhaps another reason for our lack of knowledge about cat breeds is the way we often acquire our kittens, many of which come via a friend whose queen has 'accidentally' given birth to a litter, through advertisements in newspapers and magazines, or from animal welfare societies. This has been the traditional method of obtaining a kitten, and there is still some resistance to actually paying for a kitten when many are given free 'to good homes'.

Types of kitten

There are three basic types of kitten available, as follows:

• A pedigree – or pure-bred – kitten is the offspring of pedigree parents of the same breed. The advantage of choosing a pure-bred kitten is that you will have a good idea of how it will look as an adult, and of the typical temperament characteristics of the breed.

• A kitten is described as cross-bred if both its parents were pedigree cats, but of different breeds. In this case, the kitten could grow up to resemble either or both of its parents.

• A kitten is known as a non-pedigree if one or both of its parents were cross-breds themselves. Indeed, different breeds may have been mixed over several generations, making the appearance of kittens in a litter difficult to predict before they are born.

Whichever type of kitten you choose, your main priorities should be that it is healthy and has been well cared for by its breeder. The bright eyes and glossy coat of this non-pedigree kitten are good indicators that it is fit and well.

The terminology used to describe the three types of kitten may vary slightly in different countries – for instance, a non-pedigree is often described as a 'moggie' in the UK, but as a 'mixed breed' in the USA. However, for the purposes of this book, two basic terms are used: pedigree (pure-bred kittens) and non-pedigree (all other kittens).

Types of coat

Whether you choose a pedigree or non-pedigree kitten (and many people happily keep both), the care that you need to give it will be similar. One of the major decisions that you must make is whether you would like a short- or a longer-haired cat. For instance, you may love the look of the Persian, but will you have the time for plenty of grooming and are you prepared for the amount of hair it may shed around your home?

Cats vary in their type and length of hair, and in their ability to look after their own coats. Breeds of cat are classified according to coat type as follows:

• Longhair: These impressive-looking cats have long, very full coats that require a great deal of attention to keep them in good condition. Some individuals – such as Persians with very flattened faces – may find it difficult to groom themselves thoroughly and, if not groomed daily, will end up with seriously matted coats.

• Semi-longhair: These cats have long but less full, or thick, coats than the Longhairs. They will be able to tend to their fur very efficiently themselves, although they will appreciate a little help from their owners.

- Shorthair: These cats are of course able to look after their own coats perfectly well, and need very little in the way of grooming. However, regular brushing will help to keep both the skin and the coat in top condition, and many cats also enjoy the attention.

Owner involvement

Another decision that you should make at the start concerns how much interaction you wish to have with your future kitten. We all like to have a cuddle and a game, but this can become mandatory rather than a matter of choice if you choose one of the more attention-demanding breeds such as the Siamese. If your preference lies with a somewhat quieter cat and you are happy to carry out a thorough daily brushing routine, you may decide to opt for an elegant Persian. A British or American Shorthair is also likely to be the choice of many – these popular cats are independent and self-reliant, thereby combining ease of maintenance with companionship and feline friendship.

WHICH BREED?

Although the physical variations between cats are small when compared with the huge range of body size and shape in the canine world, there are differences between the breeds in body conformation and head shape, coat length and colour, and between the various colours and patterns of coats within particular breeds, so there are plenty of options. Non-pedigree cats also come in a really beautiful array of coat colours and patterns, and nature designs some extremely unusual and pretty 'one-offs' as well as the very common colours such as black-and-white or tabby.

Breeds are maintained by only allowing cats with certain characteristics to mate with other, similar cats, or by bringing change through controlled mating so that the origin of any variations is known. Genetics is a highly complex subject, and the range even within coat colours in the breeds is

The coat-colour variations in non-pedigree kittens are almost limitless; common bi-colour mixtures such as black and white are always popular.

constantly changing. This means that, while some breeds have one coat colour, such as the 'blue' Korat (the coat is actually grey, with a silver tipping), others may have many colours (such as the Persian).

There is a good chance too that, because we select certain cats to mate, and control which genes are put into the melting pot, the disposition for certain behaviours may be passed to the kittens along with their physical characteristics. Thus when you hear that Siamese cats are vocal or that Ragdoll cats are loving, these are generalizations that may give an indication of the temperament of your chosen kitten. However, scientists agree that the differences between individual cats are still greater than the general variation between breeds.

The 50 or so breed categories that we know today have arisen in different ways: some came about naturally in geographically isolated areas, while others have been 'man-made' by further manipulating the breeding of the originals or by using one-off mutations to develop new types. For example, the Siamese developed in isolation from other cats to form the basis of the individuals we know today, yet we have introduced changes through selective breeding to produce colour varieties and alterations in body shape that we like. Breeds such as the Somali have arisen by cross-breeding (in this case, by introducing a gene for long hair into the Abyssinian), while the Maine Coon and Norwegian Forest breeds developed from a mixture of cats which, by various means, reached the USA and Norway – now their home countries.

Some breeds have come about by breeding from one or two kittens born as mutations – in other words, kittens different to the norm thrown up naturally from time to time in nature. Examples are the Devon and Cornish Rex with their sparse, curly coats, the hairless Sphynx and the Munchkin (a cat with short legs, akin to short-legged breeds of dog such as the Dachshund). Some people have even tried to breed a miniature cat, although the closest that we have come naturally to this is with the Singapura, a small- to medium-sized cat familiarly known as the Singapore drain cat, which – as legend has it – originated in the back alleys and drains of Singapore. However, an important ethical consideration here is that, as buyers of such breeds, we must ask ourselves whether we wish to create a demand for cats with no hair, short legs or other mutations, or whether we would prefer the cat to remain as nature intended: a tough, independent and agile creature that is able to hunt and to live a long, healthy life.

Cat shows

Most people are aware of a handful of breeds – notably the Persian, Burmese and Siamese – because of their distinctive looks and great popularity. However, there are many more feline breeds available and, if you are contemplating a pedigree kitten, the subject is worth some investigation. One of the best ways of deciding what you may like is to visit a cat show. In some countries, large shows and many smaller or specialist breeds shows are held throughout the year (look in cat magazines for details – see page 158). When you visit a show, have a good look around and talk to the breeders and other enthusiasts there.

It is even more important to start off with knowledge of the show world if you are intending to show and breed with your own kitten – every enthusiasm has its own rules and regulations, and its likes and dislikes, so you should get in on the ground floor and start asking questions before you obtain your kitten, not afterwards.

For additional information on some of the most common cat breeds, and their appearance and characteristics, see Chapter Two.

HOW MANY KITTENS?

Many people who are thinking of acquiring their first feline companion only consider having a single kitten, but there are many advantages to obtaining two kittens together. Although this may at first seem to mean twice the cost of feeding, neutering, vaccinations, medical expenses and so on, there are also many non-cost-related benefits, not to mention the fun to be had with two inquisitive kittens learning about the world around them.

Students of animal behaviour know that the dog is a pack animal and needs to be part of a group, whereas the cat is a solitary hunter, which explains much of their differing behaviour. However, this fact does not preclude a cat from enjoying social interaction with its own species, as owners with more than one feline can testify.

Unlike their feral counterparts, pet cats have the need – if not the desire – to hunt removed by a ready supply of food at home, and, with the time and effort of territory patrol and reproduction no longer on the agenda if they are neutered, they have even more 'spare time' to fill. Cats normally sleep for up to 60 per cent of their lives and spend about one-third of their waking hours grooming themselves, but this still leaves time for social interaction – whether this be with other cats or with their human owners.

By bringing what is still essentially a wild animal into the home, and removing many of the dangers it would normally face by feeding and tending to it, we provide the pet cat with what would seem to be a very easy lifestyle – albeit one that attempts to curb its independence to fit into our way of living. This can be successfully achieved because the cat is a very adaptable species and, as is evident in

Having two kittens can be double the fun. You will be treated to great displays of feline behaviour as they play, but taking on two kittens is something to consider carefully.

millions of homes, provides us with companionship and entertainment while still maintaining much of its wild behaviour outdoors. However, it can also mean that cats come to rely heavily on human owners for their social behaviour, a responsibility that we must be sure to fulfil.

Advantages of two kittens

It is a great deal of fun to have two kittens, and you will see much more of the feline behavioural repertoire as they play. Kittens enact the whole gamut of body language in their daily frolics, and this provides a wonderful opportunity to see just how much they can contort themselves or erect the fur on various parts of their bodies in their play-fights. It does mean that the kittens will often shoot around the house and, yes, sometimes up the curtains together, but this phase will soon pass as they grow and become heavier.

Of course, the personality of every cat is highly individual, and not all kittens are as boisterous as others. In fact, if one kitten is a little nervous and quiet, another less-inhibited kitten may help it to interact and to tackle some situations that it would otherwise have avoided. Companionship will be of particular help in those first few days on entering a new home, when all is strange and very frightening. Obtaining two kittens together also removes many of the problems of introducing a companion to the household at a later date, because, once one cat has acquired territorial attachments to both house and owners, and when maturity – even if it is neutered maturity – has introduced the additional sexual-competition factor (see opposite), it is that much harder to get two cats to share happily together.

Many cat lovers already know the value of getting two kittens – sometimes it is twice the trouble, but usually the fun factor is squared!

Disadvantages of two kittens

Obtaining two kittens certainly relieves much of the 'guilt factor' of leaving a single kitten alone all day, and makes going to work much easier on the conscience as the kittens race around the house or curl up together, oblivious of your departure. However, this cat companion-ship does raise the question in some owners' minds as to whether the two kittens will bond to each other instead of to them. This is a valid concern, perhaps more so for people who hope for a type of dog-like devotion from their cats. However, cats do seem to be able to switch from feline to human interaction fairly happily, and do not spurn our attention simply because they have been curled up with their feline partners all day. As ever, they usually make the best of both worlds and will still seek out a warm lap whenever it becomes available.

One other practical consideration for anyone wishing to buy two long-haired kittens is the extra effort that will be required to groom two cats instead of just one – this is a time-consuming process that should not be under-estimated.

Kittens from different sources

Obtaining two kittens from the same litter makes life fairly simple, but, if you would like to own one of the pedigree breeds yet cannot afford twice the cost, you could consider getting a non-pedigree cat to go with it. Make sure, however, that you are fully aware of the medical implications – both kittens must be healthy and not a potential disease risk for the other (you should discuss their ages and vaccination status with your vet to minimize any risk).

MALE OR FEMALE?

Having decided to obtain a kitten – or even two – what about its sex? If you are buying from an experienced breeder there should be no problem in ensuring that you are given a kitten of the sex you desire, but veterinary centres probably have a daily intake of Sams who come in to be castrated and leave as Samanthas (or vice versa), much to their owners' embarrassment. While it can be difficult to tell the sexes apart when kittens are tiny, it does become easier as they grow up.

Many of the differences between the sexes are shaped by hormones which dominate cats' reproductive lives. In general in the animal kingdom, it can be said that males tend to be rather more difficult to control than females and are more prone to aggression, especially during the breeding season. However, with most of our kittens we remove the influence of these hormones by having the kittens neutered before they become sexually mature (neutering is normally carried out at or before six months of age – see pages 150–3).

There is actually very little to choose between the sexes once they are neutered, and their behaviours are very similar, but what may affect your choice is whether you are introducing your new kitten into a household where there is already a resident cat. In this case, it is usually better to choose a kitten of the opposite sex to the older cat, in order to remove any element of sexual competition. They will therefore be less of a threat to each other, as this competitive drive can still have some influence even if both cats are neutered.

Similarly, if you plan to obtain two kittens together it is probably best to choose one of each sex – or two females – to avoid the risks of potential competition that would normally develop between males later on,

In a male kitten, the tip of the penis is hidden in an opening 1 cm (½ in) below the anus, with the scrotal sacs in between.

In a female kitten, the vulva is a vertical slit almost joined to the anus like a letter 'i'.

especially as they approach sexual maturity. Neutering will, of course, remove much of the difference in behaviour between males and females so this is not necessarily a vital consideration, but it could be an issue with some types and some Oriental breeds, which may some-times become more competitive with members of their own sex.

WHAT IS THE BEST AGE?

Eight weeks is the optimum age for a non-pedigree kitten to go to its new home. All kittens must by this time have encountered a broad range of experiences, people and animals, to ensure that they become confident and sociable family pets (see pages 43–4). In the UK and some other countries, pedigree kittens almost always remain with their breeders until they are at least 12 weeks old, so that they have completed their primary vaccinations (see page 87) and are litter-trained before they go out into the world.

If you already have an older cat (or if you plan to obtain two kittens), you must think carefully about the sex of the new kitten. Introductions to an older cat will also need careful planning (see pages 64–8).

If you decide to obtain a kitten from an animal welfare society, you may have less control over its age. If the kitten is more than eight weeks old, be very cautious if nothing is known about its previous history – it may not have been properly socialized (see pages 41–4), which could lead to great problems later on.

WHEN TO GET YOUR KITTEN?

It is often in the winter with the fire roaring and the family snuggled beside it that we feel the need for an addition to our homes, in the form of a kitten to curl up on our laps or to snooze in the chair. However, this may not be the easiest time of year actually to find a young kitten.

Breeding times

Most cats have their kittens in the spring or summer, when there is an abundance of wildlife on which to feed their offspring. Pet cats, of course, will be fed by their owners and could have a litter any time of year, but nature has adapted them for survival in the wild, not for the human household. If you would like a non-pedigree kitten, you should therefore bear in mind that starting your search in the spring or summer will give you the greatest chance of finding one.

Having said this, it is also true that nature can sometimes be 'fooled' by breeders in order to produce pedigree kittens at other times of the year. This is done by keeping a female intended for breeding (known as a queen) indoors in artificial light to create a constant 'day length', since it is the shortening of daylight hours that will bring a queen out of the fertile phases of her reproductive cycle and depress her ability to mate (see also pages 150–1). Some pedigree breeds also seem to have more unusual breeding patterns, so you will need to check with a breeder as to the availability of kittens.

The best time for you

Not only will you need to find out when kittens are most likely to be available, but you must also be prepared to set aside sufficient time to look after the new addition to your family. Many owners of recently acquired kittens and puppies can be heard to remark that they had forgotten what hard work it was to have a baby in the house! You should be prepared to spend at least a weekend with your new kitten, settling it in, learning about its needs and its character, and helping it with litter training if this has not already been carried out at the breeder's house (see pages 82–5). If you can have a few days at home with the kitten, then so much the better.

It is obviously inadvisable to collect your kitten just before you go on holiday, as this would mean a stay at a cattery (see pages 106–8) before the kitten has even had the opportunity to become used to your home. While there is nothing wrong in familiarizing a kitten with a cattery at which it is likely to stay in the future, it will need time to settle in and to decide where home is first.

Similarly, you should avoid obtaining a kitten just before the Christmas period, or at any other time when there may be many strangers in the house. A kitten needs consistency and care, and does not deserve to be forgotten during a period of festivity when there is likely to be considerable disruption and perhaps also the challenge of excited, noisy children. The baubles on a Christmas tree and other decorations around the house can also prove quite irresistible to an inquisitive pet so, if you do have a new kitten at this time of year, take care that it cannot reach them.

It is also unwise to obtain a kitten just before a baby is due, as the disruptions to the household can be huge and there may simply not be enough time to give both baby and kitten enough attention. A first-time mother in particular naturally tends to worry about the health of a new baby and, in the early days, may be concerned – usually needlessly – about health-related matters (see page 70), or about the kitten accidentally jumping on the baby and so on. To avoid these worries, it is best to let the baby grow up a little, and then to introduce a kitten. To the kitten, the child will then be a normal part of the household, and it will learn to enjoy or avoid as need be!

CHAPTER TWO

CAT BREEDS

This chapter outlines the size, shape, coat type and colour of some of the more common breeds of cat, as well as a few of those less often seen. It also attempts to give a general idea of the breeds' behavioural characteristics, although the variation between individual cats within a breed can still be much greater than between one breed and another.

There are three different coat types in the cat: longhair, semi-longhair and shorthair. If you decide to take on a longhair, you must be prepared to carry out a thorough daily grooming regime (see pages 96–9).

Unlike pack-orientated dogs, where humans have shaped the different breeds to do a job of work – be it herding, guarding, hunting or simply acting as companions – cats have developed as solitary hunters. They may have lived alongside us for thousands of years (see pages 110–13), but they have not been expected to perform particular tasks, or to do as they are told. The natural and excellent hunting skills of the cat have made it very useful to humans as a rodent controller, but we have done nothing to shape those predatory skills as we have done in the canine world.

However, there are some general characteristics that can give us something to go on when we are trying to decide just which type of cat we would like, and how it may be likely to behave. Although little scientific research has been carried out to date on the behavioural characteristics of different cat breeds, owners and breeders have noted specific breed tendencies, some of which do seem fairly clear-cut.

Neither the details of any particular breed 'standard' – those of shape, size and form set down by the feline authorities (such as the Governing Council of the Cat Fancy in the UK – see page 158) – nor the variations between breed standards in different countries are discussed here. If you wish to buy a kitten for breeding and showing, you may wish to contact the society or club of your preferred breed, from which you will be able to obtain much more detailed information. If you would simply like a pedigree kitten as a pet, the following information may help you to decide on the look and general characterization that you like, and therefore on the breed of cat that will best suit your lifestyle.

LONGHAIR

Persian

The Persian – known officially as the Longhair – is one of the most popular cat breeds, although its looks have changed somewhat over the years. The modern Persian is medium-sized and sturdy (or 'cobby') in build, but has a much longer and thicker coat, a flatter face and smaller ears than when it was first shown in the late 19th century. The eyes are large, round and usually copper-coloured, but they can vary from orange to green and blue.

The Persian's coat is long and luxuriant with a soft undercoat, and requires regular grooming to keep it from matting. The coat can range from 'self' (solid) colours from black through chocolate, cream, lilac and blue to white. White Persians may be orange-eyed or blue-eyed, or may have one eye of each colour. The white coat and blue eye colour can be associated with deafness, so take care when you are choosing this type of kitten.

Persians can also be bi-coloured (a mixture of white with one of the self colours), blue-cream, cameo (a white undercoat with darker shading towards the tips of the hair), chinchilla (a white coat and emerald-green eyes which look as though they have been outlined in kohl pencil), colour point (a coat pattern similar to that seen in the Siamese, with a range of coloured 'points' at the mask, ears, stockings and tail, which are darker than the paler body; this is because these areas are at a cooler temperature than the core of the body, and the hair is pigmented differently as a result), shaded silver (a white undercoat with black tipping), golden, smoke (a pale undercoat with darker tips; this cat looks self-coloured until it moves), tabby (with markings of various colours), tortoiseshell, and tortie and white.

The Peke-faced Persian, which has a very flat face and was developed in the USA, is not recognized by the Governing Council of the Cat Fancy in the UK.

In temperament, the Persian is a gentle, friendly and generally undemanding breed.

SEMI-LONGHAIRS

Balinese

The Balinese is a semi-longhaired Siamese with a silky coat. Its body is long and slender, the head is wedge-shaped and the ears may be tufted. The colour points are seal, blue, chocolate, lilac, red, cream, tortie or tabby. The Balinese is less demanding than the Siamese, but similarly lively and intelligent.

Birman

The Birman is a long-bodied cat with a rounded head and blue eyes.

Its coat is long and silky, with darker points on a pale body, and four white paws give the breed a most attractive look. The coat colours are seal, blue, chocolate, lilac, red, cream, tortie, tortie-tabby and tabby. The Birman is said to have been kept as a sacred temple cat in Burma, its country of origin, which may give rise to its intelligent, often reflective character and quiet disposition. This breed was unknown in the UK until the mid-1960s.

Maine Coon

The Maine Coon is regularly described as the biggest feline breed. However, males of up to 8.2 kg (18 lb) are at the extreme, and most are simply sturdy cats with long legs, a strong body, a long head and a squarish muzzle. The breed has a friendly and playful nature.

The coat of the Maine Coon is everything that it should be to protect the cat outside in a harsh winter – heavy, thick and waterproof.

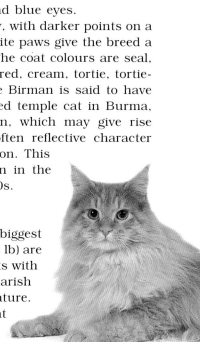

The fur is thicker around the neck, giving the cat a distinctive ruff, and its ears and paws may be tufted. The 'Coon' part of the name is thought to come from its large size and bushy tail (early American settlers thought it a cross between a cat and a racoon). The coat may be of any colour or pattern.

Norwegian Forest

The Norwegian Forest cat developed to survive in the cold temperatures of Norway, and is renowned for its great proficiency at climbing. It is strong and long with a thick, waterproof coat – which may be any colour or pattern – and a woolly undercoat.

This is probably not a cat to be kept indoors, as it is a great hunter with an independent but friendly personality.

Ragdoll

The Ragdoll is surrounded by tall tales – such as the story that the mother of the first litter was run over by a car and so produced 'floppy' kittens; or the myth that cats of this breed cannot protect themselves because they are too docile – but in fact it is simply a good-tempered, gentle cat which will often 'flop' in a person's arms like a rag doll.

This cat is fairly big, with a strong body and a flat-skulled head, large tufted paws, a beautiful bushy tail, and blue eyes which are large and oval in shape. The coat is silky and medium in length, and the fur is fairly dense. The coat comes in seal, blue, chocolate and lilac, and in three patterns: colour-pointed, mitted ('with paw tips of a different colour) and bi-coloured (white combined with any of the self, or solid, colours).

Somali

The Somali is a semi-longhaired version of the Abyssinian, its double coat being dense, fine and very soft to the touch with treble-banded ticking (each hair bears three dark bands). The coat colours of this breed are sorrel, chocolate, blue, lilac, fawn and silver. The Somali is an intelligent cat and has an extrovert temperament.

Turkish Van

The Turkish Van is a cat which seems to break the feline rules – we all know that cats hate water, but not this one. Named after the Lake Van region of Turkey, where it was first seen, this breed loves water and enjoys a swim, and it will even take to the bath if a lake is not on offer.

The Turkish Van has a long, sturdy and muscular body, a strong, wedge-shaped head and straight nose, and orange, blue or odd-coloured eyes. Its long, silky coat is described as auburn and cream. It is a friendly and intelligent cat.

SHORTHAIRS

Abyssinian

The Abyssinian still looks much as it did in the 1800s when it arrived in the UK with traders visiting from Africa, with its close-lying, double-ticked coat (each hair has two dark bands) giving a similar appearance to that of a wild rabbit. More colours – sorrel, blue, silver, chocolate, lilac, fawn, red, cream and tortie – have since been developed.

The Abyssinian is said to need company to share its intelligent and outgoing personality.

British and American Shorthairs

The British Shorthair (right) is a large cat with a sturdy body, heavy feet and a round head with small, neat ears and large eyes. The American Shorthair (opposite, top) has a larger head and a more rangy body.

The short coat of both breeds is dense and shiny. Self (solid) coat colours range from black, chocolate, blue, cream, red, lilac and white to combinations of bi-colour (white with any of the self colours), blue-cream, colour-pointed (the points are like those of the Siamese), smoke, tabby (either classic or mackerel, in various colours; the

latter has a series of lines down the cat's body), spotted (similar to the patterning seen in various wild cats), tipped (a white under-coat with various darker shades at the tips of the hairs) and tortoiseshell.

Both the British and the American Shorthair have a very friendly and affectionate temperament.

Burmese

Among the pedigrees, the Burmese is now almost as popular as the Siamese with cat owners – even in the UK, where the breed arrived only as recently as 1948. Almost all Burmese cats in existence today can be traced back to a single walnut-brown queen called Wong Mau, who was taken from Rangoon (the capital of Burma) to the USA in 1930.

The Burmese has a short, shiny, dense coat that feels wonderful to stroke. Its body is medium-sized and sturdy, and it has a rounded head and wide-set ears. In profile it has a firm chin and a distinct nose 'break' (unlike the Siamese, which has a straight profile). Coat colours are brown, blue, chocolate, lilac, red, cream, brown tortie, blue tortie, chocolate tortie and lilac tortie. The tortoiseshell Burmese is said to be the naughtiest of all the varieties, and also the most extrovert, so if you are hoping for a quiet life this may not be the kitten for you!

The Burmese is an outgoing cat and will always let you know when it is about, although it may not be quite as talkative as the Siamese. It is intelligent and enjoys human attention, liking to be involved in whatever is going on. It usually has plenty of energy and has been described as brave, athletic, humorous and capable of showing great ingenuity. Many members of the breed will retrieve balls of paper or other objects, often keeping their owners playing for hours, and take well to being walked on a harness and lead (see page 78).

The Burmese is thought to be one of the longer lived of the cat breeds, with individuals commonly reaching their late teens.

Exotic Shorthair

Just when you thought you were getting to grips with all the breeds and their various colours, the Exotic Shorthair pops up. This is really a short-haired Longhair: in other words, it has the same body shape and form standards as the Persian cat, with less of that long hair and thick undercoat to deal with. So, if you like the look of the Persian, but feel that you could not cope with all the grooming, the Exotic Shorthair may be the cat for you.

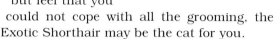

This breed is available in all the colours and colour points of the Persian, and has the same affectionate and undemanding temperament, making it a good indoor cat.

Korat

The Korat is a breed whose coat comes in just one colour – blue. It originated in Thailand, and is one of the oldest-known cat breeds. It first arrived in the UK in 1972, where it has become popular because of its quiet, friendly temperament and its pretty, pear-shaped face and round eyes, which give it a very appealing expression.

Manx

The Manx cat is another easily recognizable breed, in this case because of its tail – or lack of one. In fact, there are three types of Manx cat, each characterized by the length of tail: the completely tailless Rumpy, the Stumpy and the Tailed.

If the Manx cat were presented as a new breed today it would probably not be accepted by the cat-breed authorities because of the problems associated with breeding these cats (the lack of a tail is actually the result of a spinal deformity). Indeed, two completely tailless individuals cannot

be bred together because of this deformity, so Stumpy and Tailed cats are used for breeding, and the resulting Rumpy kittens are then sold as pets.

The Manx cat has a well-rounded body with a hopping, rather rabbit-like gait associated with hindlegs that are slightly longer than the forelegs. Its short, thick fur – which can come in any colour and pattern – needs regular grooming. Cats of this breed are generally very docile and outgoing.

Oriental Shorthair

This breed has a long, slender body shape like that of the Siamese, but has a solid coat pattern instead of the darker coloured points. It comes in a variety of colours, from self (solid) colours such as black, blue, cream, havana, red, white, caramel, fawn, cinnamon and apricot, to non-self colours such as tabby (classic), tabby (spotted), tabby (ticked – each hair bears two to three dark bands), tortoiseshell and tortie-tabby. The blue-eyed white form of the Oriental Shorthair, which is known as the Foreign White, does not suffer from the deafness common among other blue-eyed, pure-white cats; this is probably because the blue of the Siamese eye is different in genetic terms from that of non-Siamese breeds.

The Oriental Shorthair is among the most intelligent and energetic of cat breeds, and makes a very lively and rewarding pet for the right owner. Like the Siamese, members of this breed are typically vocal – with a distinctive voice that ensures they will not be ignored for long – and enjoy human attention. Individuals tend to become very attached to their owners.

Russian Blue

The Russian Blue (which really did originate in Russia) is a medium-sized to large cat with a beautifully soft double coat – the fur is like thick velvet and feels silky to the touch. It has a straight profile and whisker pads which stand out a little, giving it a very strong face. In temperament, the Russian Blue is quiet, gentle and affectionate.

Siamese

The Siamese is probably the best known of the pedigree breeds, and the beauty of its long, elegant body, fine legs and tail, and wedge-shaped head is accentuated by its colour points. However, when the Siamese first appeared in an exhibition in London in 1871, it was described as 'an unnatural nightmare kind of a cat' – probably because of its striking coat and bright blue eyes (which may have been squinting), along with a kinked tail. These defects of a kink and a squint were common in the breed at that time, but have since been greatly reduced by selective breeding. Its grace, beauty and strong personality have made the Siamese (often referred to as the Royal Cat of Siam) sought after worldwide.

The breed comes in a range of colour points, from the most commonly known seal point to chocolate, lilac, red, cream, tortie, tabby, tortie-tabby, caramel, cinnamon, fawn and apricot points.

The Siamese character is well known: these cats are intelligent and talkative, playful and outgoing, and are often described as being 'dog-like' because of their willingness to retrieve items, to walk on a harness and lead (see page 78), and even to learn tricks. However, their best trick is to train their owners to do as they are told – Siamese are not cats to be easily ignored!

Like the Burmese, Siamese cats are usually long-lived, reaching their teens with no signs of ageing and gracefully moving into old age.

Tonkinese

The Tonkinese is a cross between a Siamese and a Burmese, and was first developed in the USA in the 1960s. As both of these breeds are beautiful individually, it is no surprise that the Tonkinese is also a very attractive cat. In looks, it lies about midway between the two, and may be the ideal choice for cat lovers who prefer the 'chunkier' appearance of the more traditional-type Siamese.

As you would expect from a combination of two breeds not renowned for their reticent personalities, the Tonkinese is intelligent and interactive, and enjoys joining in with whatever is going on. It has a fine, close-lying, short coat that comes in brown, blue, chocolate, lilac, red and cream, as well as in the various torties, tabbies, and tortoiseshell and tabbie.

OTHER COATS

Cornish and Devon Rex

In the 1950s and '60s, two cat breeds originated from the south-west of England. Both are natural mutations – in other words, they come from kittens which were born into normal litters and were then made into specific breeds. The Rexes have a curly, rather sparse coat, in which the hair is fine and has a rippled appearance. It may be any colour or pattern. The coat seems to moult less than that of other breeds, and some people who are normally allergic to cat hair have found that they can live with the Rexes without problems.

The Cornish Rex (above) has a slender, muscular body and long legs, and a long, tapering tail; the head is wedge-shaped with large, high-set ears.

The Devon Rex (right) has a shorter coat than its Cornish cousin. The ears are large and low-set, giving the breed a pixie-like appearance.

The Rexes are intelligent, playful and friendly, and appreciate plenty of human attention.

Sphynx

Most cats are recognized because of their fur type or colour, but the Sphynx is an exception to this rule. Its claim to fame is that it appears to be hairless (it does in fact have a fine down of fur), so that the skin's pigmentation and pattern are clearly visible. It is a medium-sized cat with large ears and slender legs, and is gentle and good-natured.

The Sphynx is not accepted as a breed by the Governing Council of the Cat Fancy in the UK.

CHAPTER THREE

FINDING THE RIGHT KITTEN

Wherever you go for your kitten, be it a pure-bred individual from a breeder or a non-pedigree kitten from an animal welfare society, you need to know exactly what you are looking for in order to take home a healthy, friendly kitten which will be a rewarding and much-loved companion for many years to come.

FINDING A NON-PEDIGREE KITTEN

An old theory was that all female cats should be allowed to have one litter before they were neutered – to 'settle' them, or simply because it was considered a pity not to give them this opportunity. This is now thought totally unnecessary, and most owners have every intention of neutering their cats – female or male – to avoid unwanted pregnancies. However, cats grow up very fast – they can be sexually mature by five or six months of age (see page 150) – and sometimes a 'baby' female kitten finds a tom earlier than its owner had anticipated!

Picking from a litter

The unexpected arrival of many non-pedigree litters means that people often do not actually go looking for a kitten, but are asked by a friend or neighbour to give a beautiful and irresistible little ball of fluff a good home. Kittens are also often advertised, 'free to good homes', in newspapers and at veterinary centres.

If you select a kitten from a litter such as this, be sure to follow the guidelines outlined on pages 33–6 on how to pick out the best kitten for you, and how to check its health and general condition.

Pet shop kittens

It is best to avoid buying a kitten from a pet shop, and there are many reasons for this. Firstly, you will probably not know the age of the kitten, which is an important consideration (see pages 42–3). If it is on its own, you will not be able to establish the health status or character of its mother and littermates, or the character of its father (this may have a strong influence on that of the kitten – see page 37).

Another drawback is that you will not know how well the kitten is being looked after. Many pet shop kittens are taken from their mothers

All young kittens – such as this non-pedigree litter – are very appealing, but you need to choose carefully in order to end up with the right kitten for you and your family.

too early, their normal diet is suddenly changed and they are placed in a strange environment where they do not receive the care and attention that they need, and this can cause great stress and illness.

A kitten in a shop may also be housed with other individuals which are carrying disease. They are unlikely to be vaccinated (see page 87), and you could buy a kitten which not only succumbs to disease very quickly but also brings it into your home – an important consideration if you have other cats. If you must buy from a pet shop, check all these aspects very carefully, and ask for a certificate of vaccination if the owner claims that this has been carried out.

Animal welfare societies

The number of welfare societies which care for cats is vast, and they range from large national organizations to kind people who simply take unwanted cats into their homes. Although there are many cats needing good homes, do not be overcome by sentiment when choosing a 'rescued' kitten. Remember that you will become attached to it very quickly and, if you have picked out a kitten because it looks unwell and you feel sorry for it, you may well be on the road to grief. Young kittens which are unwell die very easily, so take care.

If you would like to obtain a kitten from a welfare society, find one which is well run, clean and orderly. Bear in mind that the more cats that are kept together in a small space, the greater the risk of spreading

disease (see pages 89–91). Kittens in this environment may be protected by antibodies from their mothers' milk for a few weeks, but will subsequently stand a high risk of catching a feline disease in the period before they can be vaccinated. Many responsible and knowledgeable individuals who rescue cats only take on a litter or two at a time – or find new homes for kittens individually – and ensure that their hygiene precautions and the management of the cats' environment is very strict.

Many people obtain kittens from animal welfare societies. This can be a good option, but you should be cautious when taking on an older kitten with no knowledge of its background.

If you do decide to take on a kitten from a welfare society, you will be asked questions about yourself, your home and how you will care for the kitten. A member of the staff could even visit your home. You may have to agree to neuter the kitten when it is older, to prevent more unwanted litters (see pages 150–3). You may be asked to pay for the kitten, or to give a donation towards the work of the society.

Ferals

There is a chance that you will be offered a feral kitten to home. This type of kitten will have been born 'in the wild' and lived without human interference, so it is really a wild animal. Some pet cats that have become lost or were abandoned by their owners (these would in fact be classified as strays rather than ferals) live a feral lifestyle of scavenging and hunting for a period, but will usually re-integrate into a human home if it is offered.

However, kittens born feral will remain wild if they are not introduced to humans by the age of seven or eight weeks, and even then they may be very spitty, nervous and prone to hiding away. This is because there is only a very short period in a kitten's life when it can form bonds with other species (see pages 41–4). A kitten brought up from birth in an environment with numerous people, dogs and other cats will take this as normal and accept the presence of different species in its new home, whereas a feral kitten will follow its instincts to hide and protect itself.

For these reasons, if you hope to obtain a kitten which will grow up confident and relaxed in your home with people, other animals and a busy lifestyle, you need to be sure that it has met all these situations before you take it on, or that you obtain it at a young enough age to have an influence on it. Some people do have the talent and patience to work with older ferals and gradually succeed in 'domesticating' them, but, if you are offered a feral kitten more than seven or eight weeks old, you may never have the friendly cat that you envisage.

FINDING A PEDIGREE KITTEN

When you go to a breeder for a pedigree kitten, you will obviously have already decided on the breed you would like. Most good breeders are very well informed about their particular breed – and about cats in general – and will give you excellent advice about your kitten.

How to choose a breeder

As with most specialist interests, there is a wealth of information on breeders if you know where to look for it, such as in specialist cat magazines, or from cat societies. In the UK, the Governing Council of the Cat Fancy (see page 158) is the body which registers pedigree cats and kittens. It publishes information in its own magazine and in other

Some breeders keep cats in outdoor quarters. Wherever they are, the quarters should be clean and provide the cats with a stimulating environment.

As a litter grows older, their breeder may keep them out of harm's way in a special pen or crate (see also page 49).

publications, and compiles lists of breed clubs, advisory groups, breed sanctuaries and cat shows. There are similar organizations in other countries: your vet should be able to advise you on contacting them.

Once you have selected one or more breeders, telephone them to find out if kittens are available. You may need to visit the kittens and make your choice when they are fairly young, and then to wait until they are the correct age for re-homing (in the UK, the Governing Council of the Cat Fancy recommends that a pedigree kitten is not re-homed until it is 12 weeks old, and has been vaccinated and litter-trained).

Tell the breeder whether you plan to breed from your kitten, or simply wish to keep it as a pet. Breeders sometimes have kittens which are not quite right for showing – for example, with a small marking in the wrong place (known as a 'fault') – and these are described as pets rather than breeding-quality kittens. If this does not worry you, you may be offered a cheaper kitten than one destined for the show ring. You may have to agree in writing to have the kitten neutered when it is old enough (see pages 150–3), to prevent the fault from being passed on.

One other option to buy a kitten more cheaply is to do so on 'breeding terms', where the breeder has the right to decide which stud the kitten will mate with in the future, and can then choose an agreed number of offspring. However, the Governing Council of the Cat Fancy in the UK does not recommend purchasing on these terms.

Visiting the breeder

This will give you a chance to see the kittens with their mother (and, ideally, their father, if he is kept there, as his personality will affect that of the kittens – see page 37). You will also be able to evaluate the environment in which the cats are kept, by checking whether it is warm and clean, and whether the breeder is aware of the need to keep infectious diseases at bay. If there are many cats and the surroundings are dirty, it may be wise to choose another breeder.

Equally, you should not be over-impressed by sparse, ultra-clinical surroundings, as producing healthy, sociable kittens requires attention to hygiene combined with knowledge of a kitten's social development (see below and pages 41–4). Kittens brought up in an unstimulating environment with little human contact are less active and interactive, and may always be wary of new sights, sounds or people. You must be aware of this fact when you buy a pedigree kitten, because breeders generally keep kittens until they are 12 weeks old, so the socialization process will be up to them. In contrast, most non-pedigree kittens will probably have been thrown into the fray and left to get on with life!

A good breeder should also ask you a number of questions about your house, garden, lifestyle and knowledge of cats, to ensure that you will be able to provide a suitable and caring environment for the kitten.

THE RIGHT KITTEN FOR YOU

Whether you have opted for a pedigree or a non-pedigree, choose a kitten which seems to want to interact both with you and with its littermates. It is very difficult to sum up personalities in the brief period when you are introduced to a litter – looks and colour often take prefer-ence. However, research indicates that there are different types of kitten: those which enjoy social interaction with people and other cats, and those which prefer their own company. The more owners attempt to interact with them, the more this second type will distance themselves.

Try to imagine for a moment that you are a very small kitten. So far, your only experiences of the world have been living with your mother and littermates in a cosy, quiet nest. Your human owners, a quiet couple, have been kind and considerate. They have fed you well and cared for you, stroking you gently and making gentle cooing noises. Now they have found you a new home, and it could not be more different. It is full of strange smells, noisy children, barking dogs and an adult cat which is clearly not pleased to see you – in other words, completely overwhelming. No wonder a new kitten sometimes prefers the underside of the spare-room bed to the chaos of the living-room carpet!

By trying to take the kitten's perspective (see also pages 117–21) it becomes easy to see why the experiences and environment of a young kitten during the 'sensitive' socialization period are so influential. A kitten which has never before set eyes on a dog or a young child, for instance, will find the transition to its new home much more difficult than one already familiar with them. This means that, if you have a busy family, with children, dogs or other pets, it makes sense to buy a kitten from somewhere with a similar environmental profile.

Most owners would like a loving and interactive kitten which is happy to be shown off to friends and family, and is not nervous of everything around it. Choosing an outgoing, healthy kitten from a litter is therefore the obvious first step. Remember that, while a cat's character may change over time, a timid cat is unlikely to become an extrovert.

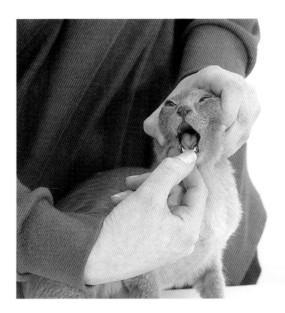

Carefully open the jaws and look inside the mouth: a young kitten's milk teeth should be clean and white, the gums pale pink and healthy, and the breath should not smell.

The coat should be clean and glossy, and the skin pale and smooth. Part the fur in places with your fingers to check for the presence of parasites such as fleas (see pages 92–4).

The eyes should be bright and clean, with no discharge. The third eyelid should not be showing in the lower part of either eye – if it is, the kitten may not be entirely well.

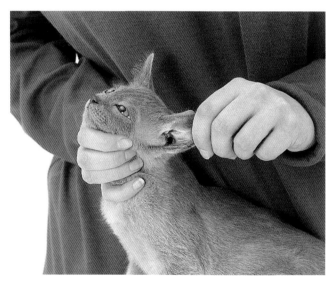

The ears should be clean and free from discharge or wax. The presence of dark-coloured wax – particularly if the kitten is scratching – may indicate ear mites (see pages 94–5).

CARRYING OUT A HEALTH CHECK

The health of your kitten is vital. Just because you have travelled all the way to a breeder's house, or because you are desperate to take a kitten home from an animal welfare society, it is important that you do not rush into a decision; instead, having picked out a kitten that you like, stand back and check it over carefully and objectively. There is nothing worse than taking home a sick kitten, having to pay for expensive veterinary treatment and becoming deeply attached to the kitten, and then losing it suddenly through illness.

No matter how good the breeder or animal welfare society, check the kitten over yourself for your own peace of mind. This is often a question of following your instincts – some kittens simply look 'not quite right', or are very quiet. You could ask your vet to come with you if you are unsure or inexperienced, and pay for his or her advice; alternatively, once you have collected your kitten, take it for a full check-up with your vet to ensure that there are no health problems that you may have missed (see pages 86–8). If your vet does come across any problems during this examination, he or she will help you to decide what to do (all good breeders of pedigree kittens should be happy to sell them subject to veterinary approval).

What to look for

The kittens and mother should all look healthy and bright, and the kittens should be lively and inquisitive. If there are any ill kittens within the litter it is very likely that – even if you choose a healthy one – it may have been infected but that the disease has not yet shown itself, so be tough. Do not let yourself be tempted by the runt of the litter, or by the little sick one sitting in the corner – this will only bring you problems and a lot of heartache.

Gently pick up the kitten that you like and check it over from top to toe. The coat should be clean and glossy, with no dry patches or dandruff. There should be no signs of fleas or other parasites (see pages 92–5) – part the fur and have a look. Check inside the mouth for healthy, pale pink gums and clean white milk teeth; the kitten's breath should not smell. There should be no discharge from the eyes or nose. The nose itself should feel cool, velvety and slightly damp, and the kitten should not be sneezing or sniffing. Its breathing should be even and not 'rattly' or wheezy.

Ensure that the kitten's third eyelid is not showing in either of the eyes (you will see this as a white membrane covering the lower part of the eye), as this is a sign that the kitten may not be entirely well. The ears should be clean and free from discharge. If there is dark-coloured wax in the ear and the kitten is scratching, it may be suffering from an infestation of ear mites (see pages 94–5). The area around the base of the tail should be clean – any sign of reddening or fur-soiling should be investigated, as the kitten may have diarrhoea. It should not be pot-bellied (this may indicate a heavy worm infestation – see pages 91–2), and should walk without stumbling or limping. If you are in doubt about anything at all, ask the breeder or a vet.

If you are happy that your chosen kitten looks healthy in all these respects, let the breeder know your final choice. If the kitten is a pedigree, you will probably need to pay a deposit. Finally, unless you are taking the kitten home the same day (in which case you will need to have made all the appropriate arrangements at home in advance – see Chapter Five), arrange the date when you will return to collect it.

CHAPTER FOUR

YOUR KITTEN'S DEVELOPMENT

Your kitten's appearance, personality and behaviour are unique – no other kitten in the world will be the same. How this individuality and these characteristics are formed is a magical combination of nature and nurture: the effect of genetics, development in the womb, and the kitten's experience of the world around it after birth.

PARENTAL INFLUENCES

Studies have shown that the personality of a kitten's father has a direct effect on that of the kitten – an interesting point when one considers that most kittens have no contact at all with their fathers, and that most owners do not even know the identity of the father! This means that a kitten born of a sociable, affectionate and outgoing father is more likely to have those qualities, whereas a kitten fathered by a nervous, anti-social cat may well reveal those characteristics as an adult itself. Of course, the mother's genetic influences will be equally important, but study of these is complicated by the fact that the mother's behaviour also influences the kittens after they are born.

Such research does not discount the added effects of the environment and the vital role of socialization on cat behaviour (see pages 43–4), but it does indicate that a kitten's genetic blueprint is highly relevant.

BEYOND GENETICS

Your kitten is also subject to physiological influences. Even while cocooned in the womb, it is developing and is affected by various factors. The normal gestation period for a domestic cat is 63 to 66 days. At only 24 days after conception, it is likely that the kitten has an awareness of touch; by day 54 in the womb, it already has the basic 'righting' reflex, which becomes refined after birth (see page 42).

During the pregnancy, the kitten is continually bombarded by the effects of hormones, nutrition and even the chemical changes caused by any stress in the mother. A nutritionally well-balanced, calm and contented mother is more likely to produce kittens which reflect this state of health, both mentally and physically. Kittens born of a severely undernourished mother may well have poorer learning aptitude, show less tolerance of other cats, and reveal higher levels of reactivity (for example, running away or showing aggression) in stressful situations.

However, these influences are likely to be uncontrollable by you as a potential owner: you may not even know about the state of the mother before she gave birth, and the father's identity may be lost in the annals of time. A kitten is rarely conceived, born and brought up in the most ideal of situations – yet the majority of kittens become happy, much-loved family pets. How is this possible? The answer is that the environment into which a kitten is born, the mother's behaviour after birth and human influences all have a huge impact on its behaviour.

THE DEVELOPMENTAL STAGES

The development of a kitten is divided into four main stages – neonatal, transitional, socialization and juvenile – before adulthood is reached at the age of about one year. These divisions are not distinct or rigid, but depend on an individual's growth rates as well as on factors such as the mother's health and welfare, and the influences of the environment.

Neonatal period

The neonatal phase lasts from birth to about 10 days of age.

Physical development At this first stage of the kitten's life, eating and sleeping are the only vital functions for staying alive. The kitten is totally dependent on its mother, and relies on her to feed it, to keep it warm and to stimulate its bowel and bladder movements by licking the area under its tail.

A newly born kitten cannot regulate its own body temperature and has little control over its limbs or body movements – it will not be able to walk for at least three weeks.

If very young kittens are left by their mother for a brief period, they will huddle together for shared body warmth.

However, the kitten can cry if it becomes separated from its mother, and by four days old it can 'paddle' short distances (for example, if it becomes separated from the warmth of the litter in the nest) using a simple 'rowing' action of the forelegs to drag itself along.

Sensory development The kitten's eyes are closed at birth. Although the ears are also covered by folds of skin, even a very young kitten will respond to loud noises by raising its head. It probably locates the teat area through a combination of warmth, touch and also the sense of smell (it is thought that a kitten follows a saliva trail, left by the mother after giving birth, to the nipples).

Feeding Once at the teats, the kitten learns to latch on to a nipple through small, innate bobbing movements of the head, known as the 'rooting reflex'. It is also born with a sucking reflex, which causes it to turn its head towards any object – such as a finger – that touches the mouth area. This reflex gradually becomes more sophisticated, and after a few days only the feel of a teat will provoke this response.

At this stage, suckling will continue for up to eight hours a day. A kitten usually weighs about 100–120 g (3½–4 oz) at birth, but this can double in the first week alone.

Behaviour Soon after birth, some co-ordination in the forelegs allows the kitten to make treading movements around the teats to stimulate the mother's milk flow. This 'kneading' behaviour is sometimes also seen in adult cats at moments of great contentment. Interestingly, a little later, the kitten will begin to purr as it suckles. This also seems to stimulate the mother's milk flow, and soon becomes a signal to all the other kittens that food is about to arrive.

A queen may decide to move her litter after only about two days in a nest site – perhaps to a safer place, but perhaps also to offer her kittens the stimulation of a more diverse environment than the safe comfort she needed for giving birth. To move the kittens, the queen grasps each in turn by the scruff of the neck before carrying it to the new spot she has chosen. Being picked up by the scruff in this way causes a reflex action in a kitten – its forelegs become limp, while its hindlegs and tail curl up out of the way. During the transportation in its mother's mouth, the kitten will appear to be temporarily immobilized, and will not attempt to struggle or make any noise (see also overleaf).

Presumably of great adaptive value in avoiding predators, this reflex action (known as flexor dominance of the vertebral musculature) continues into adulthood in many cats, making it very useful for restraint in an emergency. Some vets have even been known to grasp the skin on the back of a cat's neck with a clothes peg, creating the instant trance-like, immobile state in the cat and leaving both hands free for administering first aid.

If the queen wishes to move her kittens for any reason, she will do so by picking up each in turn by the scruff of the neck.

Transitional period
This phase lasts from approximately 10 days to three weeks of age.

Physical development In this phase, the crawling movements which were possible at the end of the first week have become more developed, and by about 17 days the kitten will make attempts to stand up, although it will remain wobbly for some time to come. The milk teeth begin to appear at about 14 days of age.

Sensory development The eyes generally open at about 10 days, although a kitten will not be able to see with clarity or accuracy until the age of approximately four weeks. At 15 days the ears are open and fully functional.

Feeding In the third week the kitten starts to experiment with eating solid food, and will spend up to one minute a day attempting to do so. It will try any food that it sees its mother eating, and this imitative behaviour has a very strong impact later on (an adult cat's personal taste preferences often stem from food that was eaten in kittenhood).

A kitten's eyes normally open at about 10 days old, but this may happen as early as the middle of the first week.

Behaviour The weaning period marks a huge behavioural step for the kitten. This is the time when the mother starts to withdraw her milk supply by spending more time away from the litter and by lying in positions in which her teats are inaccessible. In the wild this behaviour is essential for the queen's survival, as providing the litter with enough milk would now be depleting her body reserves. However, it creates frustration in her kittens, which try harder to get to the milk.

Eventually the conflict between mother and offspring is resolved, as the queen re-directs her kittens' attention to solid food (or prey, in the wild). Weaning therefore encourages nutritional independence as well as a kitten's first experience of being encouraged to resolve frustration and conflict (see also pages 128–30).

During weaning the mother begins to deny her kittens continuous access when they attempt to feed from her.

Scientific studies indicate that the time of weaning also influences the development of play behaviour. Before weaning takes place, a kitten is primarily engaged in social play with its littermates and mother. However, the onset of weaning coincides with a reduction in social play, and a marked increase in play with objects. This would appear to be in preparation for the predatory skills needed to hunt and kill prey, yet studies also show that such play is not necessarily an indicator of a cat's hunting proficiency as an adult. Hunting skills are instinctive but practice makes perfect, and having a good teacher – in the form of the mother – seems to make the difference.

Socialization phase

This lasts from about three weeks to between nine and 14 weeks of age. The end of the socialization phase varies greatly between litters, and seems to depend on the richness of the environment: a kitten born into complex and stimulating surroundings will explore them earlier, concentrating less on social play, while a kitten in a poor environment may continue to engage in social play until it is 14 weeks old.

The 'sensitive' period for socialization to humans and other animals is between two and seven/eight weeks of age.

Physical development Between the age of three and four weeks a kitten begins to gain self-control over urination and defecation, and will start to move away from the nest to relieve itself. A kitten of this age will also start to toilet in loose, rakeable litter in a litter tray. Imitation of the mother may play an important role in this behaviour.

By the fourth week the kitten will move around quite confidently, and can often run and balance well by the fifth week. However, it will be another five or six weeks until it can run, jump and leap with accuracy, balance and co-ordination.

A five-week-old kitten can groom itself – and its littermates – effectively, and this natural behaviour is vital for coat health, temperature regulation and social contact. Grooming also acts as a 'displacement' activity in cats: it seems to reduce tension

Kittens engage in a great deal of social play: this teaches them social skills and is also essential for the development of good prey-handling abilities.

and anxiety as an individual goes through a familiar, comforting and physically pleasurable routine. This may also be one of the reasons why most cats love to be stroked or petted by humans.

The so-called 'righting reflex' – which ensures that a cat lands on its feet after a fall – is fully functional after six weeks. This reflex works by orientating the head and upper body first (by twisting in the air), so that the cat faces the ground. The rest of the body is then turned in line with the upper half, and the cat literally falls on its feet. While this means that cats can often survive fairly serious accidents, it does not always prevent injuries. A fall from a great height – such as from an upstairs window – may result in broken hindlegs and/or other severe injuries.

Sensory development The kitten's hearing is fully developed at about four weeks of age, and this allows it to orientate itself and to move towards noises. Its vision will also have improved considerably by this time. The kitten is now able to judge distance and depth accurately, and so can follow moving objects by sight alone. Visual development will continue until 16 weeks.

Feeding By the fourth week, the kitten will spend approximately 25 minutes per day eating solids; this increases to about 50 minutes per day by the age of six weeks.

Behaviour The socialization phase is the time when a young kitten forms relationships with members of its own species, learning to communicate with them via body language and social signals (see pages 121–6), and also discovers how to cope with other species such as humans and dogs. In fact, this period could essentially be regarded as the 'make or break' stage in a kitten's life since, to a great extent, it determines how well the kitten will cope with life as a domestic pet in the years to come.

Social play teaches the kitten how to react and respond to the actions of other kittens, and the increased time spent on this activity tends to correlate with the mother spending less time with her offspring. Kittens tend to play in a different way from adult cats. Adult play is usually centred around a predatory-style pounce and chase, while kittens prefer 'belly-up' games, leaping and 'stand-offs'. This play between littermates is often fairly rough, and a kitten will soon learn that it has to inhibit the scale of its 'attacks' on other kittens if the violence is not to be reciprocated. Such 'attacks' therefore gradually tend to become moderated, and turn into play in the form of rushing at another kitten, and then veering away or rearing up on the hindlegs at the last minute instead of actually making contact.

Social play with the kitten's littermates is usually overtaken by play with inanimate objects – known as object play – at about 14 weeks (female kittens become particularly intolerant of their male siblings' attempts to play with them as they enter the juvenile stage). Research has shown that object play – such as chasing, pouncing, batting and scooping – stimulates cats in a very similar way to that of their natural hunting activities.

The socialization phase is also the time when a kitten needs to meet and be handled by as many people as possible if it is to grow into a suitable pet for the average home. Recent behavioural studies have demonstrated that a kitten must be handled by a bare minimum of four different people during this phase in order to be friendly with everyone whom it encounters later in life. In addition, it needs to be individually handled for a minimum of 40 minutes a day if it is to cope with close human contact as an adult.

Of course, the timing of the socialization phase – and in particular the 'sensitive' period from the age of two to seven/eight weeks – puts the responsibility for adequate, pleasant exposure to people firmly with the kitten's first owner, or breeder. A kitten must experience as much as possible of domestic life during this period, in order to be able to take everything in its stride.

What this means is that the kitten needs to meet plenty of different types of people – those with beards, glasses or wearing hats. It has to understand that people with loud voices or sudden movements – such as children – are not threatening, but are in fact pleasurable to be with. It must learn that car rides are not frightening, that to be sniffed by a friendly dog is strange but bearable, and that other, adult cats exist but are not a danger. It needs to have seen and heard sights and sounds as diverse as the washing machine on a spin cycle to people sneezing – and everything in between. There is so much to learn about life, so much that a kitten can regard as either terrifying or tolerable, and only five or six weeks in which to learn how to react for the rest of its life. This is a heavy burden of responsibility indeed, and explains why choosing the right breeder is so important.

Juvenile phase

This is the period between the end of the socialization phase and the onset of sexual maturity. Its timing can vary a great deal not only from breed to breed, but also between pedigree and non-pedigree kittens (see page 150).

Physical development By this stage the kitten's motor co-ordination and skills have improved, and muscle development and ability to balance reach a peak.

Sensory development All the senses of the adult cat – sight, the sense of smell, hearing, balance and touch sensitivity – are now fully developed in the kitten.

With the onset of sexual maturity, the vomeronasal organ (sometimes called the Jacobson's organ) may come into play. This structure – a pair of fluid-filled sacs situated directly above the upper incisor teeth – is connected through fine ducts to the nasal cavity. Its function is to provide an extremely specialized third chemical sense that is a kind of cross between smell and taste. Most often used in connection with sexual behaviour, an adult cat can sometimes be seen drawing scents – particularly the smell of other cats' urine – in through the nose, into the vomeronasal organ, to be 'analysed'. This action is accompanied by a distinctive gape, where the upper lip is drawn back and the mouth held open for several seconds. The 'Flehmen response', as this is known, is thought to be an important part of courtship, perhaps as a means of judging the receptiveness (or otherwise) of a prospective mate.

Feeding By this stage the kitten will be able to live entirely on solids provided by its owner (if it is leading a domesticated life), and no longer requires any milk in its diet. It is also now able to hunt effectively. The efficiency of the cat as a hunter does not appear to be determined by the amount of object play in which it has previously engaged, but the teaching abilities of the mother do seem to have an impact. A mother who provides a great deal of injured prey for her kittens to kill, or who allows them to accompany her when out on hunting excursions, is likely to pass on her particular hunting skills to the kittens through their observation and imitation.

Behaviour A kitten in the juvenile phase can perform almost every behaviour of an adult cat. In a natural environment, this would be the time that the kittens in a litter would normally disperse, either of their own volition or because they are ousted by their mother, who may have simply had enough of sharing her home and food with so many hungry mouths, and must conserve her strength for her next litter.

Although cats are often regarded as being solitary creatures, it is in fact quite possible – and indeed common – for them to live together in social groups. However, they are unlike dogs in that they have no strict social 'rules' or co-operative hierarchies to unite or structure a group. Instead, group living and cohesion are more likely to depend on the amount of space and resources – particularly food – that are available, and also on individual character and tolerance. This may perhaps account for the differences between a home in which several cats live in harmony, and another where just two cats cannot tolerate living together. Personality types, previous experience as a kitten, socialization and the

During the juvenile phase a kitten continues to learn the full repertoire of adult behaviour, especially prey-handling skills and how to interact with other cats.

success of introductions to people, other cats and a range of animals (see Chapter Six) are also likely to influence whether a kitten will get on well with other felines in the same household. For instance, a kitten that is hand-reared from birth and isolated from other cats will never fully learn that it *is* a cat, and so will react aggressively or defensively with others of its own species.

CHAPTER FIVE

PREPARING FOR YOUR NEW KITTEN

If you choose a pedigree kitten from a litter, there may well be an interval of several weeks before the kitten is old enough to come home with you, and you can use this period to make the necessary preparations for its arrival. Even if you plan to choose and collect your kitten on the same day, you will need to have bought some essential items and ensured that your home is as safe and secure as possible.

BASIC EQUIPMENT

A kitten does not require vast or expensive arrays of accessories. It is also worth remembering that although there are huge numbers of products on the market – from toys to luxury baskets – their cost does not necessarily reflect their value. The following is a list of the basic items that you should obtain before your new kitten arrives; you can of course add to these later on as you wish.

A carrier

You will need a secure carrier for bringing your kitten home. There are many types of cat carrier available, from cardboard and wicker to solid plastic and plastic-coated wire mesh. Whichever type you choose, you are likely to keep the carrier for the duration of your kitten's life. If it is to be a show cat it will travel in the carrier regularly; otherwise you may only need it for trips to your vet or boarding cattery.

The carrier that you choose needs to be safe, secure and cleanable. Make sure that the lid fits tightly, as kittens have very supple bodies and can squeeze through unbelievably tiny spaces. It is best to avoid using a cardboard carrier, which may break if it becomes damp with urine and may be scratched through by a very persistent cat. You will also have to buy a new carrier every time it is soiled, as you will not be able to disinfect it.

The easiest carriers to use are the plastic-coated mesh, top-opening variety. Not only are these secure and washable, but you will be able to lift out your kitten easily. With a front-opening carrier – especially one with plenty of 'foot holds' – if the occupant decides not to come out it can scratch at the hand coming through the opening, or brace itself on either side of the exit so that getting it out becomes quite a challenge!

Feeding bowls and food

Whether they are stainless steel, plastic or ceramic, feeding bowls should be sturdy with non-slip bases. Saucers are not ideal, as kittens often try to climb on to them with messy results. As a minimum, you will need one bowl for food and another for water. Many owners like to leave dried food out for their cats to help themselves as they wish during the day; if you also provide canned (moist) food, you should put this in a separate bowl. Keep all bowls for your kitten scrupulously clean, but be sure to wash them separately from your own crockery for obvious reasons of hygiene.

Feeding bowls are available in various materials, and must be sturdy with non-slip bases. Shown here (clockwise from top) are stainless-steel, plastic and ceramic bowls.

You will also need a supply of suitable food for your kitten. Changing a cat's diet – particularly at times of stress, such as when moving to a new home – is often responsible for causing stomach upsets and diarrhoea, so it will be best to keep to the food with which the kitten is familiar for at least a week until it has settled down with you (you could ask the breeder or previous owner for a diet sheet and perhaps also a little of the kitten's food to tide you over when you first bring the kitten home). If you decide subsequently to change the kitten on to a food of your own choice, you will need to do so very gradually to avoid digestive upsets (see also pages 79–82).

A stable plastic bowl will be ideal for your kitten's drinking water; you should clean and re-fill it every day.

A litter tray and litter

Many different designs of litter tray are now available. Some kittens prefer open trays while others seem to like the security of the hooded variety, particularly if they feel vulnerable to disturbances such as assaults from other pets while using the tray.

The type of litter that you choose will also depend on your kitten's preference to some extent – for example, the majority of cats seem to prefer fine-grade, loose material to clumps or pellets. The ease of disposal of the litter, as well as its weight when you carry it home from the shop, may also influence your choice (see pages 82–5 for further details on litter trays and types of litter). At first you should use the same litter used by your kitten's breeder, as this will be familiar and therefore help the kitten to feel more at home. If you wish to change to another type of litter, do so gradually.

A bed

It is essential to provide your new kitten with a bed of its own. This can be as rudimentary as a cut-down cardboard box with a warm blanket or soft cushion inside, or a more luxurious commercially made model, but its main purpose will be to provide a much-needed sense of security on your kitten's first nights away from its old home.

A comfortable bed will provide your kitten with warmth and security. It should be placed in a quiet position, away from the general bustle of the house, so that your kitten can rest in peace and without disruption.

The bed should be as warm and draught-free as possible if it is to win favour in your kitten's eyes: fake-fur or 'sheepskin'-type fabric placed in the bottom of the bed will make it warm and inviting. It should also be a sanctuary away from other pets, children and the general hustle and bustle of the house. Your kitten will need to sleep a great deal in its early weeks and must be able to rest securely and without disruptions.

Encouraging your kitten to sleep in its own bed from the start will also help to prevent a take-over of your furniture or beds.

A contented cat will often 'knead' the area in which it is about to curl up, and this pummelling can be hard on more delicate or easily caught fabrics. They also need to be easy to clean, as bedding can be a breeding ground for fleas (see pages 92–4). A plastic bed will be easy to wipe clean, but remember that the blanket or cushion in the base still needs to be fully washable. Wicker has a tendency to attract dust and is also more difficult to clean, so this should be avoided if possible. Most cushioned fabric beds can be machine-washed, and some are made with a hood to make them feel very 'safe'. Bean-bag beds for cats are also now widely available, but beware the inquisitive kitten which chews a hole in the cover – the thousands of polystyrene beads inside may make an entertaining night for the kitten, but will give you a lot of work in the morning!

A 'hooded' cat bed is very cosy and gives its occupant (or occupants) greater privacy. As with any other type of bed, it must be fully washable in order to reduce the risk of flea infestations (see pages 92–4).

Finally, a 'cradle' designed to hang on a radiator is often a favourite. This may be particularly useful if your kitten is a little nervous or in a busy household, as it will feel more secure resting above ground level. Of course, the warmth from the radiator beneath also gives this type of bed a magnetic attraction for most discerning cats.

A crate or pen

Using a kittening pen or indoor crate for your kitten's first few weeks will be a great time- and stress-saver for you, and will also serve as a nice secure den for the new arrival. It will be impossible for you to watch over your kitten's every move throughout the day, or to be sure of its whereabouts all the time, and – however thorough your safety precautions (see pages 53–7) – a kitten can chew electric wires, escape from the house or even drown in the time it takes just to answer the telephone or to open the front door. A crate or pen will also make introductions to other cats and dogs much easier and less traumatic for all concerned (see pages 64–9).

Ideally, the crate or pen that you use should be large enough to allow your kitten to move about freely inside – the kittening pens used by many breeders to raise their young kittens are perfect, and you may even be able to borrow one of these for a few weeks. A dog-transit cage (also often described as an indoor kennel, or crate) will also be suitable for your kitten's first weeks with you, and will probably be large enough to accommodate a kitten, its bed, a litter tray and a bowl of water if you need to leave the kitten inside for longer spells. A cage of this type will be fairly costly to buy, but you may be able to rent one from a breeder or your vet.

A kittening pen or crate provides a secure den for a kitten's first few weeks in its new home. The pen should be sufficiently large to allow the kitten to move about freely; a few toys placed inside will provide entertainment.

Should your kitten become lost, a safe, elasticated collar will help to identify it. When fitting a new collar, make sure that you can slip two fingers underneath it.

A collar

It is essential that your new kitten becomes used to wearing a collar, with identification attached, right from the start. Even if the kitten is to live an indoor existence, accidents can and do happen – a kitten can slip out through the smallest opening, and identification becomes even more important if an escapee is unused to being outside and fending for itself. A collar and identification will also mark your kitten as a well-cared-for pet, while cats which go walk-about without collars are often re-homed by unwitting neighbours who believe that they are looking after a stray animal.

The collar that you choose must be of the safety variety, incorporating a piece of elastic that will allow the kitten to wriggle free should it become caught up. Identification can be either an engraved disc, a small barrel with the details inside, or a plastic label holder. Make sure that this is not too heavy for your kitten to carry, that the collar is not too tight (you should be able to slide two fingers beneath it) and that the skin does not become irritated. Your kitten may scratch at the collar at first, but should soon become used to it. Some collars have a reflective strip or are fluorescent, for extra safety on roads in low-light conditions.

Some owners attach a bell to their cats' collars to warn birds of their approach. However, the efficacy of these collars is questionable. Some cats simply learn to keep their heads very still while stalking prey and then pounce at the last minute to avoid sounding the bell; others seem highly irritated by the noise of the bell, which is very understandable for animals with such sensitive hearing.

Permanent identification As an alternative to a collar, it may be possible to have your kitten permanently identified with a microchip. This tiny device – the size of a grain of rice – is painlessly injected under the skin using a special needle, and the kitten's identity is then logged on to a national computer database. Should the kitten become lost, a scanner can be used to read the unique identity with which the microchip is programmed. The disadvantages are that there is no way of telling – just by looking at a cat – whether it has a chip implanted, and no guarantee that the person who finds the cat will know to take it to be scanned. However, many animal welfare societies now check for implants on 'lost' cats, and a general awareness of the technique is slowly growing. If you are interested in having your kitten identified with a microchip, ask your vet for further information.

Identification tattoos for cats are also available, although this method is less popular and the marks can become blurred over the years.

A scratching post

This is a piece of problem-prevention equipment for the home. It is a natural part of a cat's behavioural repertoire to scratch on trees, wooden fence-posts or other surfaces – generally wooden – while it is outdoors. Scratching has several very important functions. It removes the outer surface layer of the claw, revealing a sharp new point underneath (which is essential for a perfected predator); it also spreads secretions from glands between the footpads, signalling to other cats that the area has been used by this particular cat. A cat scratching in front of another cat seems, too, to be a rather assertive gesture, used to demonstrate that the cat is marking out its territory.

A sisal post (available from pet stores) is a source of fun for young kittens, as well as providing a scratching facility. Ensure that the post is properly mounted on a secure base.

As scratching is such a natural behaviour, it is sensible to provide a practical outlet for it, rather than sacrificing the end of your sofa or the Chippendale furniture. A scratching post can be a log from the garden, or a shop-bought post wound with sisal. Posts impregnated with catnip (see overleaf) are also available. It is best to avoid a carpet-covered post, which will look, feel and smell just like the carpet in your home, unless you are happy for your living-room to become one giant scratching post! This type of post may also harbour fleas (see pages 92–4).

If you watch a cat scratching outdoors, you will see that part of the ritual is to stretch up high and pull down, to achieve a really good pull on the claws. For this

Scratching is a natural part of the cat's behavioural repertoire. Even if you plan to give your kitten access outdoors, you must provide a scratching post indoors – a log like this is ideal.

reason, you should ensure that your kitten's indoor scratching post is sufficiently tall – approximately 50 cm (20 in) high – to allow the kitten to stretch up to it, even when it is fully grown. The post must also be stable so that it cannot topple over when in use.

De-clawing The claws are sometimes surgically removed from kittens' forepaws to prevent them from scratching in the home. However, this practice is totally unacceptable to the governing bodies of vets and to cat-behaviour specialists in Europe.

You may like to consider very carefully the implications of de-clawing for your kitten – the pain that will be caused by the procedure, the use of an unnecessary anaesthetic, and the loss of its claws for climbing, hunting, and so on – before you decide to go ahead with surgery. Bear in mind, too, that simply providing a suitable, specially designated scratching post in the home will usually remove the necessity to curb the kitten's natural behaviour in this way.

Cats will play less as they grow older, but still enjoy a game – and play is essential for an indoor cat (see pages 72–3).

Toys

You should have ready a selection of safe toys for your kitten, to exercise its body and its mind. Many toys are now available for cats, but the simplest types are often the most enjoyable, and you will only need one or two at first. Even a screwed-up piece of paper or a length of string will provide cheap and fun entertainment for your kitten.

Catnip Many of the toys available for cats are stuffed or impregnated with dried catnip. This herb has an interesting effect on many cats (although about 50 per cent of cats do not respond, and kittens under eight weeks old are unlikely to do so). Catnip (*Nepeta cataria*) – also known as cat mint – contains a chemical called nepetalactone, which has mild hallucinogenic effects on the cat's brain. Its soporific or excitatory effects are shortlived, non-addictive and harmless.

A cat's characteristic response to a toy stuffed with catnip is to rub, chew and roll over it, and to miaow. Those cats which do respond to the herb can go into a 'trance-like' state for up to 15 minutes, and they certainly seem to enjoy the experience.

Grooming equipment

No matter what its coat type, it is essential that your kitten becomes accustomed to being groomed from an early age. While short-coated breeds or types are likely to be able to groom themselves thoroughly, some of the flat-faced, long-coated breeds will require help, in the form of careful, regular grooming.

However, a grooming routine is not only about the health of the coat – it is about establishing a relationship between you and your kitten. Friendly cats groom each other to maintain social bonds, and we can do the same. Grooming will also accustom your kitten to being touched with an object, and to associate pleasant connotations with it. This will make visits to the vet less traumatic, as the use of equipment such as a stethoscope on its body will seem much less frightening.

A wide range of grooming equipment is available for use on cats (see pages 96–9). If you are unsure of which tools are suitable for your kitten's coat, ask your vet or a professional cat groomer for advice.

HOME SAFETY

As with many traditional sayings, 'curiosity killed the cat' is probably based on some truth – cats are naturally curious creatures, and kittens even more so. They are full of mischief and, like the young of any animal, are inquisitive and adventurous because that is how they learn about the world. However, this can mean that they get themselves into trouble in numerous ways, from climbing on to dangerous machinery or chewing poisonous plants to falling from high places or simply getting well and truly stuck in inaccessible places.

Try to distract your kitten if it shows particular interest in a houseplant, and encourage your children to do the same. If the kitten persists, you may need to move the plant out of reach, and you should certainly do so if you suspect it could be poisonous (see page 56).

While you may not be able to prevent all such accidental happenings – and your kitten will inevitably manage to do the one thing that you have not thought about – you can remove, lock or make safe many of the obvious potential dangers.

Household hazards

When you first bring your kitten home, you should try to think from its perspective (see pages 117–21). Not only do you then have to look up from kitten height (and it is amazing what you see from that angle), but you also need to have thought about those high-up places that an agile little kitten can reach. Small, dark holes seem to attract kittens, so check chimneys, holes in the floor, gaps in skirting boards and even under the bath before your kitten arrives.

Even if you plan to allow your kitten outdoors, you will need to keep it in for two to three weeks until it is used to your home and has had its primary vaccinations (see page 87), so ensure that everyone in the house knows that things have to be kept shut. Washing machines and tumble driers feature regularly in terrifying tales about kittens rescued halfway through the first wash or just before they overheat. Close

Some plants in the garden – such as the Laburnum *shown here – are poisonous to cats. Most cats do not eat much plant material, and cases of poisoning by this means are very rare, but it will be wise to prevent access to such plants if possible.*

all windows or other obvious escape routes, and block off access to awkward areas such as behind the oven.

Kittens can also easily become shut in cupboards, fridges and freezers, having just 'popped in' to investigate the contents while your back was turned. Always discourage your kitten from jumping on to the cooker or near the kettle, for obvious reasons. If you have a 'cable chewer' – and some cats do seem to enjoy getting to grips with plastic covers on cables – make sure that you turn all electric appliances off at the wall at night or before you leave the house.

Some cats' toys can even be dangerous to a kitten, which could chew off and swallow eyes, loose squeakers or the whole toy if it is small. Make sure that any toys you buy are strong, well made and suitable for a young kitten.

A tiny mouth can pick up, chew and swallow all sorts of small items that you may not have noticed. Sewing thread with a needle attached, and elastic bands, are high on the list of reasons for visits to the vet (backward-pointing barbs on a cat's tongue mean that, once taken into the mouth, an item such as a length of sewing thread can be extremely difficult to spit out).

Climbing is, of course, a favourite pastime for a young kitten, and there is probably a lot of truth in the much-quoted stories of Siamese cats and shredded curtains. However, it is not only the

A number of our common household plants – such as this umbrella plant – are poisonous to cats. Your kitten is unlikely to show any interest in plants, but you should remove them to be on the safe side.

Siamese kitten which will climb anything at hand, and most kittens will persevere with this activity until they become too heavy or until the curtains fall down – whichever comes first!

Of course, your kitten needs to learn about its own abilities and limits, and most falls do not cause any damage. Having said this, a fall from a kitchen dresser or other surface on to a hard tiled floor could cause injury, and you should take your kitten for a check-up straight away if it seems unwell or to have hurt itself. Cats are fairly good at righting themselves during falls from a reasonable height (see page 42), but remember that a cat *is* just a cat, not a mythical animal able to drop from a great height without coming to any harm. Indeed, vets now recognize what has been labelled 'high-rise syndrome' in cats – injuries commonly sustained by falling from a few storeys – so make absolutely sure that any high windows are secure, covering them over with wire mesh if necessary (see page 72).

Digitalis, better known as the foxglove, is another potentially poisonous plant. Your kitten may encounter this growing in the wild, but fence off any plants in your own garden.

Poisonous plants

Many of our household and garden plants are poisonous to cats, with consequences varying from a mild stomach upset or burning of the skin to instant death. Cases of serious poisoning by plants are actually very uncommon, since cats do not usually eat much plant material except some grass and herbs (see pages 52 and 74). However, an inquisitive or bored kitten may start to play with and chew at a harmful plant, so never leave your kitten unattended in a room with a plant that you know to be poisonous – put the plant somewhere else until the kitten is older and wiser.

Take care, too, if you buy a bunch of fresh flowers from the florist. Some of the prettiest of these – such as the cornflower, delphinium, hyacinth, iris and monkshood – are poisonous, so keep your kitten well away.

In the UK, the Horticultural Trades Association has drawn up a Code of Practice so that plants known to pose a risk are labelled (if you live outside the UK, find out whether there is a similar scheme in operation – your vet may be able to advise you).

Other poisons

Some human medicines such as aspirin and paracetamol are highly toxic to cats, so always keep them stored away safely, and never give your kitten human medication except on the advice of your vet. Some foods – such as onion, cocoa and an excess of liver or fish – can also be poisonous to cats.

You must be sure to control your kitten's access to any poisons in your garage or greenhouse – such as herbicides (sodium chlorate and paraquat), fungicides (pentachlorophenols, or PCPs), insecticides (pyrethrins, pyrethroids, organophosphates, carbamates and organochlorides) – by keeping them safely locked away when they are not in use. You should also be very careful to keep your kitten away from any lawns or flowers treated with chemicals for at least 48 hours, just to be on the safe side.

Slug pellets containing methaldehyde can easily be eaten by a kitten if they are scattered on the garden, so you may wish to let the slugs have a feast while your kitten is small, or perhaps to choose an alternative method of controlling them.

It really goes without saying that rat- or mouse-baited food or pellets (these include rodenticides such as warfarin, and also the related substances colciferol, strychnine and bromethalin) should not be left lying about anywhere within reach of your kitten – or indeed of children or any other animals – at any time.

Always keep car anti-freeze in a safe place – preferably on a high shelf in the garage – as its sweet taste seems to be attractive to some animals. Make sure, too, that fuels and wood preservatives are not able to leak out where your kitten could stand in them or contaminate its coat (coat contamination is a common source of poisoning, as the affected cat is very likely to lick at its coat in an attempt to rid it of the substance).

If at any time you think that your kitten may have ingested a poison, or has a poisonous substance contaminating its coat or skin, you will need to take prompt action and consult your vet immediately for advice (see page 95 for further information).

Outdoor hazards

Once your kitten has completed its primary vaccinations (see page 87) and can go outdoors, it will face a multitude of dangers that you will obviously have less chance of controlling than those inside your house. Roads can be a major problem, and, although you can reduce the risk somewhat by keeping your kitten in at night, to a great extent you will have to hope that the kitten learns how to cope with all the potential dangers for itself (see also pages 75–6).

Another possible problem can arise when an inquisitive kitten which is learning to hunt tries to catch wasps and bees, especially if the insects are trapped against a window. The kitten may be stung as a result of these endeavours, but this does not usually cause any long-term damage and the kitten will certainly learn by its mistakes. A kitten which enjoys hunting frogs may also occasionally pick up a toad instead and be treated to a mouthful of a vile-tasting slime, causing it to salivate and shake its head frantically to try to get rid of the taste. However, this is not usually dangerous, and the kitten will soon learn how to tell a toad from a frog, or to avoid both!

In some countries, snake bites are a potential danger (in the UK, the adder is the only poisonous snake), although dogs usually tend to be bitten more often than cats. If you do live in a 'danger area', your veterinary centre is likely to keep a supply of the necessary antidotes.

CHAPTER SIX

BRINGING YOUR KITTEN HOME

When you first bring your new kitten home you will need to decide how to organize its equipment, how to settle it in, and how and when you are going to introduce it to other members of the household – human or animal. Just how you manage all these aspects can have a major influence on your kitten's confidence and future harmonious relationships, so it is very important to get them right from the start.

COLLECTING YOUR KITTEN

The day you collect your kitten will be one of the biggest challenges of its life. It is unlikely ever to have been in a carrier, let alone been in a car, so you must ensure that it is safe, warm and secure. Line the carrier with newspaper to absorb any urine, then add some washable bedding or (ideally) a piece of bedding from the kitten's old home to make everything seem less strange. Gently lift the kitten into the carrier, and secure the lid.

A secure carrier (see page 46) is a vital piece of equipment for transporting kittens.

Ask the breeder, owner or animal welfare society to give you a diet sheet containing details of the kitten's current diet and mealtimes. You should also find out what type of litter has been used, and where the kitten has been accustomed to sleeping. Ask whether the kitten has been wormed and vaccinated (see pages 87 and 91–2); if the latter, ask for the vaccination record card so that you can pass it on to your vet.

If you have bought a pedigree kitten, make sure before you leave that you have its pedigree certificate, and that the kitten has been registered with the appropriate organization. If you wish to show your cat, you will also need to arrange for a transfer certificate or registration document to show the change of ownership.

Travelling home

Do not feed the kitten just before the journey, in case it turns out not to be a good traveller. If the journey is to be a long one, you should provide a litter tray.

If you are travelling by car and the weather is warm, offer water at regular intervals and NEVER leave the kitten inside without adequate ventilation. The temperature inside a car can build up rapidly, and overheating can be fatal. Place the kitten's carrier in a footwell, or on the back seat secured with a seatbelt, so that it cannot be catapulted forward should you have to brake suddenly. The kitten may well urinate on the way home because of the whole new frightening experience, so place something waterproof under the carrier. If you are travelling a long distance, it may be useful to pack some wet wipes in case the kitten makes a mess. If you prepare for the worst, you are bound to have a trouble-free journey!

The kitten may make an awful noise and cry pitifully on the way home. However, try not to worry: if it is warm and secure it can come to no harm, so concentrate on getting home safely and quickly. Covering the carrier to darken the interior may help to calm some kittens. When you get home, ensure that all doors and windows are shut tightly before you let the kitten out of the carrier.

YOUR KITTEN'S FIRST NIGHT

Kittens vary in their responses to spending the first night in their new homes. A few simply saunter in with a street-wise swagger and take over the dog's basket, but most need time to familiarize themselves with their new surroundings. Cats feel most secure in a small, warm environment, and your kitten may feel somewhat afraid if simply placed on the floor and expected to take everything in – do not forget how gigantic furniture and people must seem to a tiny kitten.

Ideally, you will have prepared a small, warm and cosy place containing your kitten's bed, where the kitten will spend its first night with you. This could be a crate or pen (see page 49), or simply a special area that

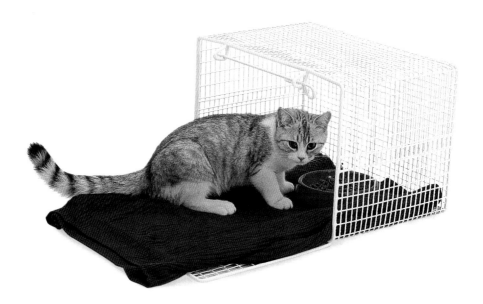

If your kitten dislikes being put in its carrier, try leaving the carrier open on its side, lining it with some soft bedding, and feeding the kitten inside from time to time so that it becomes accustomed to it.

the kitten can call its own. Allocating a small area in this way has several advantages. Your kitten will be out of the way, and so not overly disturbed by the hustle and bustle of people going to bed or getting up in the morning. It also means that you will have a good night's rest, knowing that the kitten is somewhere secure.

If you have brought a piece of bedding from the kitten's old home, place this in the bed to offer an olfactory reminder of its mother and littermates in this strange environment. Offer your kitten a little of the food to which it is accustomed, and fill up its water bowl. Your kitten should also become used to wearing its collar from the start, so gently put this on, ensuring that it is sufficiently loose for you to slip two fingers beneath it.

Remember that your kitten will need a chance to relieve itself. Gently lifting it into the litter tray every few hours before bed will help it to learn where the tray is and remind it to go to the toilet. (If your kitten has an 'accident' elsewhere, you must be sure to clean it up very thoroughly – see page 85.) Place the tray where the kitten can reach it during the night, but a good distance away from its bed and food.

Most kittens are only too happy to fall into an exhausted sleep on this first night, but a few do cry or become restless. Offer a little vocal comfort if necessary, but try to avoid smuggling the kitten under your duvet unless you want to continue this practice for the rest of its life!

Encouraging the kitten to adapt to your waking and sleeping hours is a sensible routine to establish from day one. Felines are naturally crepuscular – they are usually most active at dawn and dusk – but this does not mean that they cannot adapt to a different regime. Cats are perhaps more at risk of being hit by a car if they go out at night, and are also more likely to be involved in fights with other cats during evening and night-time periods. Keeping your kitten in at night but allowing it out during the day may be a good compromise between safety and stimulation in many circumstances (see also Chapter Seven).

After a long night's slumber, most kittens wake refreshed and ready for the new day. This may be early, particularly if the kitten has not eaten for some time. Try to encourage use of the litter tray immediately after waking, and also after eating. Your kitten will now be ready to start exploring its new environment.

VISITING YOUR VET

It is a good idea to make an appointment for your kitten to see your vet at an early stage. You could arrange this for the day you collect your kitten, but, with all the new experiences that the kitten is already having to face, it may be more sensible to wait until the following day.

This visit will allow your vet to examine your kitten thoroughly to ensure that it is not suffering from any developmental problems, and to vaccinate it and give an initial worming dose if necessary (if your kitten is a pedigree, it should already have been vaccinated – see page 87).

If your kitten does need vaccinating, it will not be fully protected for seven to 10 days (although it may still have some natural immunity to disease, passed on by its mother), so, if you have other cats in the house, you may like to keep them separated from the kitten for this period. In any case, the introductions between them should only take place very gradually, as described on pages 64–8.

SETTLING IN

Your kitten will probably be keen to explore its new surroundings, but take things slowly. Your supervision of this process should be not only practical but enjoyable, as it will help to strengthen the bond that is already forming between you and the kitten. Introduce your kitten to one new room at a time. Talk reassuringly, and allow the kitten to investigate new objects, sights and smells at its own pace – the smaller the space to be explored, the braver it is likely to be.

Try not to panic if your kitten jumps down behind the sofa or wants to explore under the sideboard – the worst thing you can do is to chase it around the room or drag it from under an object where it was resting briefly. If you do need to retrieve the kitten quickly, try luring it out by pulling along a piece of string in front of its nose or calling it for some food. Again, this creates good habits for the future. Provided that you have closed all windows, blocked off any escape routes and taken other sensible precautions, the kitten should not come to any harm.

HANDLING

Kittens tend to fall into two quite distinct groups: those that like to be stroked and given plenty of tactile affection by people, and those that like to play. This usually means that members of the former group will also take to being picked up and handled without any problems, while those in the latter group will need a little more practice at being handled in this way.

All cats and kittens are very well equipped to demonstrate that they are unhappy about being picked up, and may employ their claws and teeth to defend themselves before trying to run away. Even cats which like to be picked up, and gently held, tend to want to be there

To pick up your kitten, gently scoop it up under the chest with one hand while supporting its hindquarters with the other.

just for brief periods (and then only if they know and trust the person concerned), so you should aim to build up your kitten's confidence gradually.

The correct method for picking up your kitten is to scoop it up under the chest area with one hand, while supporting its hindquarters with the other. If you need to carry the kitten, keep your hand under its chest with your fingers between its forelegs, then close your arm into your side so that the kitten's weight is supported by your body. This will leave your other hand free to hold the kitten's head gently, or to restrain it gently by the scruff in an emergency.

Some cats learn that an excellent way to gain attention is by leaping on to their owners from a height, or by jumping on to their laps with

Carry the kitten by keeping your hand underneath its chest and your fingers between its forelegs, and support its weight next to your body.

all claws extended. It may be difficult, but the only way to extinguish this sort of obnoxious behaviour is simply to get up immediately and walk away without looking at, talking to or touching the kitten. It must learn that only initiating attention gently will achieve what it wants.

When introducing children to the kitten, sit them on the floor and then allow the kitten to investigate them in its own time. Encourage the children to stroke the kitten gently.

FAMILY INTRODUCTIONS

The next important step is to introduce your kitten to all the other residents in the house. Even if the kitten has already been used to living with another dog, or with an adult cat, do not assume that it will immediately accept your pets as well. Nor, indeed, should you assume that your pets will welcome a new kitten wholeheartedly. A little time spent preparing the animals for a harmonious life together at the start of the relationship really will be worth the time and effort.

Introducing children

As we all know, children are not the same as adults – they move, talk, sound and even smell different. Caring for pets and learning about their needs, likes and dislikes fills a vital and educational niche in many children's lives, but they do need to be taught how to care for their pets, and how to handle them gently and in a non-threatening way. If your kitten has been brought up in a household full of children, it is unlikely to react fearfully when it meets the younger members of your family. However, if it has come from a quiet, adult-only household, meeting children for the first time may be quite a shock.

Introductions should always be gradual, gentle and very quiet, as any sudden movements or unexpected loud noises are likely to scare the kitten. It is often better to ask a child to sit down on the floor and wait for the kitten to approach him or her to investigate. Ask the child to offer a small food treat and then to stroke the kitten very gently in areas where you know it likes being touched, such as on its back.

Discourage children from picking up the kitten because, especially if it is wriggling, they may easily squeeze it too hard around the abdomen and put it off being carried for life. Instead, encourage the kitten to climb on to a child's lap and remain there briefly to be petted or given a morsel of tasty food. The kitten should never be restrained during these encounters, and children need to be taught to allow the kitten to walk away freely if and when it wishes.

Encourage the kitten to climb on your child's lap to be petted, but never force it to do so or you may frighten it and make it reluctant to approach the child the next time. Never allow children to chase after the kitten or to grab at it.

Similarly, you must prevent all children – particularly toddlers – from chasing your kitten. The sight of a fleeing tail seems too much for some children to resist, but is a sure way to put the kitten off a child for some time to come. Equally, the kitten should be able to rest in its favourite spot or in its bed without being pestered, as nervousness and fearful behaviour are fuelled by lack of sleep and unpredictable attacks. Naturally, children want to explore their new pet and to establish a relationship with it, but poking it in the ear or trying to examine its teeth while it is asleep is not the best way to do so.

Having said all this, if the introductions are carried out sensitively, most children and cats become the best of friends. Many kittens bond very quickly with the youngsters in a household, and seem happy to play with them, curl up with them and 'help' them with their homework!

Introducing an older cat

You may decide to get a new kitten when a previous cat has died, leaving another by itself, or when your present cat is getting on in years. Alternatively, you may simply want to provide an adult cat with some feline company – typically, owners of one loving pet cat who decide to get another do so not for themselves, but as a companion for their pet! It is therefore somewhat ironic that an adult cat may have different ideas about a new kitten, and may not be at all pleased at its arrival.

Think about meeting someone new yourself. Would you rush into his or her home, sit on the furniture, lie on the beds and eat his or her food without even being asked? If you did, you would be unlikely to be invited back. Meeting another person for the first time requires social rules to be observed. We shake hands, smile and keep our distance, and such conventions give us time to sum each other up before forming any kind of relationship.

The same principle is true for a domestic cat, which needs time, space and social rules to discover that the other party is not a threat to itself or to its resources. These elements need to be controlled – simply bringing a new kitten into the house, placing it on the floor and expecting the cats to 'get on with it' may result in hissing, growling, spitting or a punch-up behind the television set, and will not augur well for a good future relationship.

So what is the best way to shake hands and smile in cat language? Carefully, is the answer. Not many cats will instantly welcome a feline 'intruder' into their territory, so it is up to you to make both kitten and adult cat feel as secure and comfortable as you possibly can. It is also vital that you prevent the kitten from being chased, cornered or otherwise assaulted. The ideal way to achieve this is to use a kittening pen or indoor crate (see page 49). Such protection works to the benefit of both cats. With the kitten confined in a pen, the adult cat has the opportunity to investigate, to take in the kitten's scent and to assimilate the fact that it is here to stay without feeling that its food, resting places or

Introducing a kitten to an older cat must be carried out very carefully, or it may lead to conflict. Using a pen or crate (see pages 66–7) will prevent the cat from chasing the kitten, and allow calm investigation.

territory may be threatened. Equally, the kitten remains secure. It is also prevented from running away – which could well trigger an attack by the adult cat – and from disappearing under the spare-room bed for a fortnight while it regains its confidence.

Keeping the kitten in a pen or crate at first also means that both cats have a chance to see and smell each other, but with a tangible barrier between them. This means that they are not forced into unnatural social contact with each other, but can sum each other up at a distance. Of course, the protective bars also mean that the kitten will be safe if the adult cat does decide to launch an attack. In turn, you will not become injured while trying to separate the warring factions, but will be able to intervene without confrontation. If a pen or crate is not available, a plastic-coated wire-mesh carrier (see page 46) makes a good alternative, and will allow all-round vision.

Always supervise both cats during the introductions. Watch the body language of each closely, and try to spot the danger signs that one may be about to attack. Generally, flattened ears, a low body posture and wide, staring eyes with dilated pupils indicate fear. A stiff body, a 'pounce' posture, a fixed stare with narrowed pupils and a lashing tail all show tension and the threat of aggression. Cats often 'freeze' like this in novel or frightening situations, and it usually pre-empts a 'fight or flight' response. If it becomes necessary to interrupt the cats' behaviour, use a remote interruption – such as a sudden noise – but try to pretend that it has not come from you. The aim is to make the cats think that their own behaviour caused the interruption, making them less likely to repeat it.

The step-by-step instructions given here should help you to introduce your new kitten and cat with the minimum of fuss. However, only time will tell whether these careful preparations have really paid off. Despite the best intentions and great care, some cats never learn to curl up together, wash each other behind the ears or become great friends. Personality types play a great part in all social interactions – human and feline – and it is impossible to ensure that all people, or all cats, will love each other. Sadly, friendship can never be guaranteed.

Stress-free introductions, step-by-step

Remember that all cats are different. Some may require only a brief period of introduction; others may take longer to accept each other.

1 Accustom the kitten to spending short periods in the pen, crate or carrier. Initially, you should place this somewhere above ground level – such as on a table – so that, when the time comes, both cats can see each other but are not forced into direct eye contact on the floor.

2 Bring your adult cat into the room. Make sure that it feels secure by talking to it and favouring it with your affection all the time that it is being non-confrontational. Ignore the kitten for the time being, as this will help to ease any 'jealousies' over the new arrival. Give your kitten affection and contact when the other cat is not around to see it. In the cat's presence, your kitten will probably prefer to be ignored rather than be forced into a jealous confrontation by your attention.

3 Allow the adult cat to investigate the kitten more closely. If it decides to depart to the nearest shelf to examine the newcomer from a distance, accept that this is your cat's way of coping. Never try to force a meeting

between cats, because they will need to establish a relationship in their own time. Introductions like this should be brief and positive. A few minutes of controlled, gentle introduction, several times a day, will be far better than long, tense periods of confrontation.

4 If possible, employ a 'remote' distraction to interrupt any signs of aggression between the two cats. Making a loud noise by dropping a bunch of keys is usually enough to achieve this, provided that you catch the intention rather than a full attack.

Once you have carried out the initial introductions with the kitten in the pen, reverse the situation by placing the older cat inside. The body postures of this pair show that they are still unsure of each other, and will need more time to adjust.

5 With the kitten still confined, feed both cats – at opposite ends of the room – with some extra-special food (cats are more likely to eat when relaxed, so this will be a useful indicator as to their emotional states).

6 Gradually move the adult cat's food bowl closer and closer to the kitten's pen or crate. Watch for nonchalant body postures in both cats – a willingness to eat in close proximity will indicate calmness in one another's company.

7 Move the pen around the room, and then around the rest of the house. Place it on floor level and feed the cats close together again.

8 In between these short, sweet introductions, keep the two cats apart. Play with your kitten in the other rooms of the house to ensure that its scent is as widespread as possible in the older cat's territory. In a natural situation a new cat wanting to join a group would 'visit' intermittently when the other cats were absent, to leave its smell for the others to detect; this allows gradual familiarity without confrontation.

9 Do not be in too much of a hurry to allow the cats a face-to-face meeting. As part of the process, it can be helpful to place the existing cat in the pen while the newcomer is free to wander in the room.

10 When you feel that they are ready, allow the cats to meet in one room, with the door closed. Prepare for this first 'free' meeting carefully. Delaying both cats' mealtimes so they can be fed together with some extra-tasty food often helps to defuse the situation. Place the bowls some distance apart and stand by with a means of interrupting any antagonistic behaviour, just in case. Make sure that the established cat has a place of safety to jump up to if it feels threatened.

11 Graduate to supervised meetings between the cats in other parts of the house, allowing the kitten greater freedom (if you have a cat flap, remember to shut it first!).

12 Once you are confident that the cats are happy with each other, leave them alone for short and then longer periods, until you no longer need to supervise them.

Introducing a dog

Contrary to popular myth, dogs and cats can become great companions, greeting each other, resting and even playing together. This kind of positive relationship is usually the outcome of broad early experience and good socialization for both species, but can also be achieved by careful and patient introductions.

If you are unsure as to how your dog will react to a kitten in the household, it will be a very good idea – and may also save you a great deal of worry in the long run – if you carry out a little research beforehand. For example, some breeds or types of dog – such as some greyhounds – may never cope

A pen or crate also comes in very useful when introducing a dog. You may need to confine the kitten for the first few days or even weeks when the dog is about, until you are sure that they are used to one another.

Even a Corgi can look big to a kitten. This situation should be avoided: the kitten has arched its back and is hissing, which could provoke an attack.

with the temptation of small quarry in the house. In such a case, it may be sensible to let your dog spend some time with an older cat that is quite used to being with dogs, before deciding to bring home your own kitten.

Think too about your dog's character. In possibly stressful or unfamiliar situations, does it tend to show high excitement, intense frustration or even fear? Consider the reality of having a kitten, confined to the house for the first two or three weeks, being trailed around by your panting, ever-hopeful pooch. Think about how tolerant the dog will be of a newcomer investigating its food, its toys and its bed, bearing in mind that your kitten will get everywhere once it feels secure in its new environment. If your dog is likely to be upset by the kitten's activities, you will need to take the introduction very gradually to build up confidence on both sides.

Most dogs chase cats because they are excited by the thrill of the hunt, rather than because they actually intend to cause real bodily harm. Keeping the kitten secure and unable to run away is therefore the best policy in the early stages of introduction. Confine the kitten to a large pen or crate (see page 49) for the first few days or even weeks while the dog is about, to allow each animal to sum the other up and to cope with the new smells, sights and sounds with the protection of bars between them.

Once you are happy that the dog and kitten are used to one another's presence, short and frequent meetings carried out under your close supervision – just as when introducing another cat – are required. Only allow the animals access to one another once they appear to be completely relaxed together. For these first meetings, keep the dog on a lead and make sure that the kitten always has an escape route available, and that it knows where this is.

Your kitten and a new baby

Cats and babies together seem to have created more urban myths than any other combination of animal and human. Some health visitors and even a few doctors seem keen to perpetuate tales of woe surrounding pets and the new addition to the family, but, as with so many issues in life, common sense is all that is actually required. Indeed, there are so many health issues to worry about with pregnancy that it is important to keep them in perspective. Domestic cats offer no more potential risks than any other pet in the average household, and basic, sensible precautions will eliminate those risks altogether.

Expectant mothers are warned about a barrage of health risks, particularly from infection. *Toxoplasma gondii* is a protozoan parasite which can pass to humans (a cat may carry the parasite, having eaten infected wildlife, and pass it via its faeces). This means that it is sensible for a pregnant woman to wear gloves when gardening and when emptying or cleaning litter trays – or, of course, to ask someone else to do it.

However, cats are not the sole source of toxoplasmosis: it can also be transmitted via undercooked meat or vegetables grown in contaminated soil. If you are concerned about the risks, you could ask your doctor to carry out a blood test to show whether you are immune to the infection (immunity means that there is no danger of passing the infection to a foetus; lack of immunity simply means that you have not been infected previously, thus making sensible hygiene precautions a priority).

Keeping your kitten away from work surfaces on which food or bottles are to be prepared, as well as regular hand-washing after handling the kitten, are basic necessities in any household.

Once the baby is born, common sense is again the order of the day. Parents are often concerned by stories suggesting that a kitten may climb into the cot or pram and suffocate the child by lying on it, but this is very unlikely. Cats do like to snuggle into small, warm areas, and a human-orientated cat may want to curl up with the new member of the family, but basic precautions mean that for the very short time that a baby is unable to turn over or move itself, there should be no need to worry. Ensuring that the kitten is not left alone in the same room as a very young baby, or fitting a cat net (available from baby-care stores) over the baby's pram or cot will offer peace of mind.

Your kitten may cope with the arrival of a new baby in a number of ways. Some cats seem to want to be involved, sniffing the baby and its equipment. Others take themselves off and want nothing to do with the strange creature. Whichever option your kitten chooses, prepare it for the baby's arrival by thinking ahead. If you have developed a very close bond with your kitten, cool the relationship slightly before the baby's birth, so that it will not be such a shock to the kitten when it is demoted by the amount of time that a new baby demands. Learning to cope without constant contact will also mean that your kitten is less likely to associate the new arrival directly with any reduction in attention.

CHAPTER SEVEN

YOUR KITTEN'S LIFESTYLE

The idea of keeping a cat indoors throughout its life may seem very unnatural to many people. However, if you live in a large town or city, the risks of allowing your kitten to go outside will be fairly high. Even on country roads with little passing traffic, cats seem to manage to get run over and are injured or killed, and it is thought that about 40 per cent of feline deaths are caused by such accidents. Many of these cats are young – often under one year old – and not quite 'street-wise'.

Some cats – particularly of the quieter and less active breeds (see Chapter Two) – take to indoor life quite happily, but they need plenty of mental and physical stimulation.

You may feel that your kitten has to live as nature intended and to take its chances outdoors, but some people, having suffered several losses, decide to keep their cats indoors. As a compromise, you could limit the kitten's outdoor access to your garden by means of fencing, installing an enclosure or taking the kitten out on a harness and lead.

The information given here discusses the practicalities of all the different options, and gives tips on how to tackle some of the possible problems that may arise.

KEEPING YOUR KITTEN IN

Many cats – particularly breeds with a placid temperament, such as the Persian – will take to indoor life quite happily. However, just as some humans are very much the outdoor type while others are happy to stay in, if you keep your kitten indoors you will have to judge over a period of time how well it is coping with the restriction. If you decide to take the indoor option, you should do so from day one. While a cat that is kept indoors from kittenhood can learn to go outside, it would be very unfair to make an outdoor cat stay in and would be likely to cause great frustration. You must therefore be clear in your own mind as to how you wish to keep your kitten before you bring it home, bearing in mind the following potential problems.

If you live in a flat above ground level, or if you wish to keep your kitten indoors for any other reason, you may need to make your home fully 'cat-proof' by fitting mesh on windows or balconies. Bars are another option, but remember that a young kitten can squeeze through the smallest gaps.

• The cat is a natural hunter, and has great energies and abilities to be used in this pursuit (see pages 113–16). If your kitten is not allowed to venture outdoors, it could become frustrated and develop behavioural problems such as scratching furniture or indulging in wild bouts of running around the house.

• The lack of exercise may cause your kitten to become overweight if you do not pay very careful attention to its diet.

• The kitten may become bored, and also lonely if you are out all day.

• It may become overreactive to changes within its small territory (your house), and therefore unable to cope with novelty – whether in the form of people or of objects brought in.

• There will be a much greater dependence on you for stimulation and activity, and a risk of over-attachment.

• If your kitten does get out, it may be disorientated and will not have any 'street' skills. If you keep the kitten in a high-rise flat, the dangers of a fall resulting from an attempt to escape are obvious.

• If you have only one cat, it may be very difficult to introduce another one at a later stage into your first cat's restricted territory, as there will be no neutral ground to which either party can retire.

Minimizing problems

You can take active steps to reduce or eliminate many of the above problems by the following means:

• Keep your kitten entertained. A solitary cat kept entirely indoors will often centre its waking and active time around the comings and goings of its owners, so you will have to spend time interacting with it and catering for its hunting and social needs. This is especially important with some of the more 'dog-like', socially demanding breeds such as the Siamese and Burmese, which form very strong attachments to their owners. Indeed, some individuals may even begin to over-groom or self-mutilate due to the stress of being left alone with insufficient stimulation. You must therefore be continually creative and produce new toys and games to keep your kitten exercised – both physically and mentally. Kittens and cats love newspaper 'tents', cardboard boxes and paper bags, not to mention the various play centres and climbing frames that are now commercially available.

• Monitor your kitten's food intake to ensure that it does not put on excess weight, either through lack of exercise or due to over-eating because of boredom. Make the kitten 'work' and forage for its food by placing dried cat titbits in, under or behind objects to encourage it to be active and to simulate 'hunting' activity.

• Try to ensure that you have regular visitors and that life is not too quiet – especially when your kitten is small – because this is what it will come to see as normal. As the kitten's whole world may consist of two or three rooms in a flat, it is important to avoid hypersensitivity to change, and human or animal visitors can potentially introduce huge novelty in the day-to-day environment.

• Your kitten will need to act out its normal behavioural repertoire in your home. One of these natural and important activities is scratching. Even an outdoor kitten – which may well choose a tree in the garden or a special post for this – should have a scratching post in the house, and this is essential for an indoor kitten unless you are happy for your carpets and/or furniture to suffer. (For detailed information on scratching posts, refer to pages 51–2.) Let your kitten play around the post, and drape toys over it for the kitten to swat at so that it becomes used to the post and to climbing around it. Then gently lift the kitten's front paws and rub them against the post to introduce the idea of what to do. This will also deposit some scent from the glands between the kitten's footpads on the post, and so encourage it to use the post again.

• Try to accept that your house may not always stay looking at its best, especially when your kitten is at the 'hurtling around the walls and up the curtains' stage. Put away any precious ornaments, even if they are fairly high up – you need to imagine that you have a toddler who can fly! Choose a litter tray big enough for the kitten to scratch about in and become used to – the hooded type may be better than an open tray, as this will prevent spillage of the litter. These trays also often contain air fresheners, to help keep smells at bay.

• Have two kittens instead of one right from the start. Another cat will bring change and interaction, and is highly preferable if cats are kept permanently indoors. It will also help to reduce your sense of guilt at leaving one kitten on its own when you go out. Having two kittens will relieve you of some of the burden of providing stimulation and exercise, as they will happily wear each other out playing and then collapse together in a heap (see also pages 13–14).

• An outdoor cat will nibble on grass and herbs as part of its diet (one reason for this may be that it assists in the regurgitation of hair balls). You should provide grass indoors (seed kits are available from pet shops), and perhaps catnip (see page 52), thyme, sage or parsley. You can even grow cereal grasses such as wheat and oats in a potting mixture. Sow every two to three weeks so that there is always a fresh supply for your kitten.

• Invest in some good claw clippers designed specifically for cats (see page 100). Your kitten's claws may not wear down as quickly as they would do if it walked on hard surfaces outdoors, and long claws also have a tendency to become snagged in carpets and upholstery. If you are not confident about cutting your kitten's claws, ask your vet or a professional groomer for a demonstration of how to restrain your kitten and use the clippers correctly.

Grass and herbs form a small but important part of the cat's natural diet outdoors, so you should provide a regular supply indoors for your kitten. Seed kits are available from pet stores and garden centres.

• Ensure that your home is completely 'cat-proof', especially if you live several storeys up. Put mesh over the windows if necessary, and train everyone in the family to keep all external doors shut. An inquisitive and bored kitten will be able to squeeze through a very small hole, or may work at an edge until it gives way.

LETTING YOUR KITTEN OUT

Giving cats the freedom to roam outdoors is to most people the natural course of action, and will allow them to lead active and stimulating lives. The cat is one of the most successfully adapted hunters in the animal kingdom today, and its shape, size and personality have developed accordingly. Most cats will continue to hunt – and sometimes to eat their prey – even when plenty of food is offered to them at home (see pages 113–16), and many owners feel that this very natural activity must be respected.

A safe open window is one way to provide outdoor access for your kitten whenever you wish; alternatively, a cat flap fitted in a suitable door or window (see page 77) will be a very good option.

However, the following are just some of the potential dangers that an outdoor cat may face on its daily excursions:

• Traffic on the roads – the risk of your kitten being involved in an accident will obviously be greater the nearer you live to a road and the busier it is, especially at night when the kitten may be 'blinded' by car headlights.

• Your kitten may be injured in an encounter with a dog, with a wild predator (such as a fox) or even with a person.

• It faces the possibility of infection with a number of serious feline diseases when meeting other (mainly feral or uncared-for) cats (see pages 89–91); the risks involved here will depend to some extent on where you live.

• There will be a risk of catching disease (such as toxoplasmosis – see page 70) and worms (see pages 91–2) from eating infested prey.

• The kitten could be affected by eating poisoned prey.

• Fights with other cats could lead to injury.

• The kitten could become shut in someone's outbuilding or garage, or stranded in a tree or on top of a roof.

• The kitten could be regularly taken in and fed by someone else, and could eventually decide to move in with them instead!

Minimizing the risks

The 'natural' cat, allowed unlimited access outdoors in a safe rural environment, has perhaps the best life of all, and is happy to sunbathe during the day and to hunt at night.

You will reduce the risks of allowing your kitten outdoors by taking the following steps:

• Let your kitten out during the day but perhaps keep it in at night, which is a more dangerous time for cats to be outdoors because of the presence of other, wild animals and traffic on the roads (see previous page). A reflective or fluorescent collar (available from pet shops) is a good idea, especially in the dark winter months. Dawn and dusk are the most common times for cat fights to take place, so make sure that your kitten is indoors at these times.

• Encourage your kitten to come inside during the busiest times on the road – such as the rush hour in the morning and evening – perhaps by making these its regular feeding times.

• Ensure that your kitten is protected against all the infectious diseases for which vaccines are available (your vet will advise you on this; see also page 87).

• Worm your kitten regularly. This is especially important if it is a prolific hunter, as roundworm eggs eaten by earthworms, beetles, rodents or birds may in turn infest the kitten (see also pages 91–2).

• Ensure that your kitten is wearing a collar with identification details, or has had a microchip inserted or a tattoo made (see pages 50–1). If someone finds the kitten wandering about, or injured or trapped in an outbuilding, he or she will then be able to contact you more easily.

• Have your kitten neutered, as the risks to entire animals are much greater than to neutered ones. An unneutered tom may wander for long distances and will be much more likely to fight other cats over territorial rights, causing greater risk of disease; an unspayed queen may become pregnant (see also pages 150–3).

Letting your kitten out for the first time

All kittens must stay indoors for a period when they first move to their new homes. Even if you will allow your kitten outdoors, you must wait until it has had its primary vaccinations (see page 87). If your kitten has already been fully vaccinated by the time you collect it, you must still keep it in for a minimum of two to three weeks so that it can become familiar with and bonded to its new home. The day of 'freedom' in the outside world can be nerve-wracking for owners. Cats can climb over most garden fences, and even the best-laid plans can go awry when a kitten finds a tiny hole and decides to squeeze through it. If you do not have a garden, or fencing, it may be sensible only to allow your kitten out on a harness and lead at first (see overleaf and pages 138–9).

Prior planning of the first excursion will help to direct your kitten's behaviour. Make the excursion early in the day so that if your kitten does decide to go on a wander it will have plenty of time to return before dark, and make sure that it is hungry. If you plan to allow it out first thing in the morning, encourage it to use the litter tray, but do not feed it. Cooking some food with an alluring odour – such as fish – may whet the kitten's appetite so that it will be keen to come back inside to eat.

When you are ready, open the door (or cat flap), step outside and encourage your kitten to follow by calling it and crouching down. Wait with the kitten all the time it is taking in the new surroundings. Walk with it around the garden, talking encouragingly all the time, and spend a few minutes playing with it or watching it explore. It is sometimes said that a kitten should be carried out into the garden and then placed on the ground, but cats have scent glands between their footpads, and it is important that they can make a scent trail back to the door. After some time, encourage your kitten to follow you indoors again, using the same strategy as before. Feed the kitten immediately with the delicious food you have prepared, then play a game together or allow the kitten to rest.

Over a few days your kitten's confidence about venturing outdoors will increase, and this is when basic 'recall' training is very useful. If your kitten has learned to come when called (see pages 133–5), it will be happy to come back in for a tasty treat or a meal, even if out of sight.

Fitting a cat flap

If you plan to allow your kitten outdoors, you may well opt for a cat flap. This could simply be a hole in a door or window, covered with plastic to keep out draughts, or a custom-made hinged flap which swings in both directions. A two-way locking device will give you some control over your kitten's movements. If other cats in the neighbourhood are likely to come into your house, a magnetic cat flap is a good idea. Your kitten will then wear a magnet on its collar, which acts as a 'key' for the flap. However, a great many owners now use these magnets, so if you live in a very cat-dense area you may wish to buy an electronic cat flap which will open solely in response to your kitten's personalized electronic key.

OTHER OPTIONS

As a good compromise between confining your kitten permanently indoors or leaving it entirely free to come and go as it pleases through a cat flap, you could allow it limited access outdoors by adopting one of the following measures.

Using a harness and lead

You could train your kitten to walk on a harness and lead, so that you can take safe walks into your garden or in a park together. However, while some cats – notably the Siamese and Burmese – will take well to this, others will not. If you take this option, you will need to train your kitten very carefully to accept the use of a harness (see pages 138–9).

If you cannot offer your kitten free access outdoors but would like to give it some fresh air, walking it on a harness and lead may be one possibility; this can be a good compromise between allowing your kitten to roam outdoors and keeping it indoors full time. However, accustoming a cat to wearing a harness outdoors requires slow and careful training, and some individuals – such as the Burmese (shown here) and the Siamese, which show more dog-like characteristics – may take to the experience more readily than others.

Fencing your garden

Making your garden secure is, in theory, the best solution to having a kitten and keeping it safe, although – depending on the size of the area – this can be an expensive option. What is practical for one garden may not work for another, but it should be possible to create a safe haven in at least a part of the garden.

To make an area kitten-proof you will need a fence at least 1.8 m (6 ft) high. You will need to add the actual escape-prevention system – ideally, wire mesh – at the top of the fence, horizontally or at a 45-degree angle, and extending for at least 50 cm (20 in). Fit plastic collars around any trees to prevent your kitten from climbing up.

Building an enclosure

Another option is a purpose-built enclosure. These can be bought from specialist suppliers (look in cat magazines for details – see page 158), or you could build one. In either case, you must provide shelter from bad weather and shade in hot weather. There should also be a covered area with a litter tray. Finally, add some entertainment – such as a tree trunk to climb and scratch, and some toys, which should be regularly changed – so that your kitten has a stimulating and enjoyable environment.

CHAPTER EIGHT

FEEDING AND LITTER TRAINING

Some owners firmly believe that feeding a kitten involves no more than simply opening a can or a bag of dried food, but when, where and what you feed your kitten can actually make a vital difference to its general health and well-being. Before you consider exactly what you would like to feed your kitten, it is therefore worth taking a moment or two to learn about its special nutritional requirements. Your kitten's toileting habits should also be an important consideration, and providing a suitable litter tray inside your house and teaching the kitten to use it correctly are two of the most basic necessities of good cat care.

A young kitten grows rapidly, and needs specially formulated, good-quality kitten food if it is to turn into a well-developed, healthy adult cat.

FEEDING YOUR KITTEN

Cats have evolved to become highly efficient hunters and, because of their success in feeding themselves on prey, they have not needed to rely on vegetable matter as a source of nutrition. They do, however, require very specific forms of nutrients found only in animal tissue (examples are vitamin A and niacin). They also need high levels of dietary protein with the correct balance of amino acids. For instance, the animo-acid derivative taurine is vital for a cat's eyesight, and this must come directly from an animal source – it cannot be manufactured from other materials.

Like humans and most mammals, cats use protein in food to build body tissue and carry out 'repairs', and for other biological actions such as making hormones. However, they also use protein in the way that we use carbohydrates – as a source of daily calories, or energy – so the type, quality and proportion of protein in their diets, which can only be obtained from animal tissue, are very important. Certain fats must also be provided directly in the diet from animal fat in milk, meat or fish. In short, cats are what are known as 'obligate carnivores' – they must eat meat and cannot live on a vegetarian diet.

When to feed

When a pet cat feeds itself by hunting it is unlikely to kill prey large enough to allow it to eat only once or twice a day, as most catches will be small rodents or birds. Cats are more naturally 'snackers', and will eat 10 to 20 small meals a day.

If you give your kitten dry food on an 'ad lib' basis, you will notice it returning to the bowl many times during the day for a quick top-up, rather than working its way through the food at one sitting. Cats fed on moist food do tend to eat bigger meals (this type of food dries out quickly and is more likely to go off if left uneaten, so your kitten may choose to eat more when the can is freshly opened and the flavour, taste and smell of the food are at their most potent), but most would probably prefer small and frequent meals to one large bowlful given at the end of the day. In fact, cats often do not let us get away with infrequent feeding and demand more every time we go into the kitchen.

A kitten needs small, frequent meals in order to be able to ingest and digest enough nutrients to grow rapidly, and must therefore be fed much more frequently than an adult cat. When you first get your kitten at eight to 12 weeks of age it will need to eat about five meals a day. If you are out during the daytime, one way to manage this is to provide dry food, which can be left out so that the kitten is able to help itself. If you prefer to use canned (moist) food, you

Give your kitten small meals at frequent intervals, rather than larger amounts once or twice a day. With time, the number of meals can be reduced.

may like to invest in an automatic feeder – this is a dish in which the food remains covered until a pre-set time, when the lid opens and allows the kitten access to it.

By the time your kitten is six months old – and about 75 per cent of its full size – you can reduce mealtimes to twice a day. (If you are feeding dry food on an 'ad lib' basis, your kitten will obviously continue to decide how many meals it wishes to eat every day.)

Where to feed

You should feed your kitten in a quiet place where there will be no competition from other cats and no likelihood of the food being stolen by a dog, and where there will be no other interruptions. Be sure to place your kitten's feeding bowl well away from its litter tray (see pages 83–4).

Commercially produced kitten and cat foods are available in three forms: moist (above), semi-moist (below left, top) and dry (below left, bottom).

What to feed

Making any sudden dietary alteration can cause a stomach upset, so for the first few days keep to the food to which your kitten is accustomed, before changing over gradually to another food if you wish.

It is important to feed a diet that has been formulated specifically for the rapid growth period of a kitten's first few months of life. Most of the major food manufacturers make a kitten food designed for the first six months of life. Choose a good-quality one which suits your kitten – in other words, the kitten should enjoy eating the food, look well on it and not suffer from stomach upsets.

If you dislike the idea of feeding a commercially prepared food and would like to feed your own diet, bear in mind that it can be very difficult to get right the vital balance of nutrients and energy content, and that putting together a home-made diet for your kitten will be very time-consuming. Cat nutrition is a complex science – you will need to feed a wide range of meat and fish, supplemented with all the necessary vitamins and minerals – and the results can be haphazard, especially at a time when your kitten's body is demanding very specific nutrients for healthy growth and development.

If you are worried about any aspect of feeding, or you are concerned that your kitten is not growing and putting on weight as it should do, ask your vet for further advice.

Drinking water

The ancestors of our domesticated cats were semi-desert-dwellers, and this has given our pets the ability to conserve water efficiently. If you feed your kitten on a canned moist food, it may not drink a great deal because most of the water that it requires will be provided by the food (moist foods usually contain between 60 and 85 per cent water, compared with 5 to 12 per cent water in a dry food).

An average adult cat requires a minimum of about 150 ml (¼ pt) of water per day. As you cannot know exactly how much your kitten is taking in with its food, you must always keep a bowl of clean, fresh water available so that the kitten can adjust its intake to suit itself.

Milk

Cats and weaned kittens do not require milk as part of their diet, and certainly not as a substitute for water. Indeed, soon after a kitten is weaned it loses the ability to digest lactose, a sugar found in milk. This is why some cats cannot tolerate cows' milk, and may suffer from stomach upsets if they are allowed to drink it. Even if your kitten can tolerate milk, it is inadvisable to give it if the kitten is prone to suffering from digestive problems.

LITTER TRAINING

Whether or not you intend to allow your kitten outside once its primary vaccinations are complete (see page 87), you will need to keep it indoors for at least two to three weeks so that it gets to know your house as its home, and also as the place to return to when it starts to explore the great outdoors (for advice on letting your kitten outdoors for the first time, refer to page 77).

You will therefore need to provide a litter tray for the interim period, or in the longer term if your kitten is to live entirely indoors, so what type of tray and litter should you choose, and how should you teach your kitten to use them?

A simple open litter tray is the type chosen by most owners. It should be fairly deep and large enough for a grown cat to turn around in easily.

Types of litter tray

Litter trays for cats range from the simple open variety made of plastic to a covered tray with an air freshener in the hood. Your kitten may be quite content with the open type – especially if it is only for a few weeks – but many prefer the privacy of a closed tray in the longer term (for advice on preventing problems associated with litter trays, see pages 143–4).

Some trays are very shallow, but cats like to have quite a deep litter – at least 2.5 cm (1 in) – to scratch up, so one of the deeper types of tray will ensure that the litter does not end up all over the floor. The tray should also be big enough for your kitten to turn around in easily.

Types of litter

When your kitten first comes home with you, try to use the cat litter with which it is familiar, as the kitten will associate that substrate with toileting. You can then gradually change to a new variety if you wish. There are four basic types of cat litter: re-usable litter (this usually consists of wax-covered corn husks), from which solid waste is removed and the litter then washed; Fuller's earth, which is based on clay; lightweight clay litter, which has a consistency like sand; and wood-based litter, which is made of highly absorbent sawdust or paper pellets.

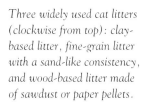

Three widely used cat litters (clockwise from top): clay-based litter, fine-grain litter with a sand-like consistency, and wood-based litter made of sawdust or paper pellets.

Some of the litters come with added deodorizing chemicals or air fresheners to reduce the smell that may escape if a litter tray has become a little too well used. However, it is much better to clean a tray more frequently than to try to mask the smell. In addition, the footpads of some cats – particularly those which live permanently indoors – can be fairly soft and sensitive, and the chemicals have sometimes been known to irritate their feet, so keep an eye on your kitten if you use this type of litter. Some cats may also dislike the strong smell of the chemicals and be dissuaded from using the tray.

The finer litters may stick to your kitten's feet, so it is a good idea to put a mat by the exit of the tray to catch the pieces. Likewise, the contents of an open tray are much more likely to land on the floor if the kitten is a little over-enthusiastic when covering up its urine or faeces, so you may want to put down some newspaper around the tray.

It is possible to use newspaper as 'litter', although this will not be particularly absorbent, and the ink may come off on to your kitten's feet where it may cause harm and also be walked around your home. Another potential problem is that your kitten may come to regard any newspaper lying around the house as fair game for toileting purposes!

Positioning the tray

You must place the litter tray in a quiet part of your house. Cats feel quite vulnerable when toileting, so you must help your kitten to feel secure and not in danger of being unexpectedly disturbed. Do not place the tray near the kitten's food and water bowls, or near its bed, as cats would naturally move away from such areas to use a latrine.

If you have a dog or a toddler in the house, be warned that both are likely to find the litter tray utterly irresistible, which may affect its positioning. Wherever the tray, your kitten must be able to gain access to it 24 hours a day.

Cleaning the tray

Do not change the litter too often at first – perhaps once every two or three days – as the smell will help your kitten to learn that this is its latrine area. (If more than one cat is using the tray, you will obviously need to clean it out more frequently.) A litter scoop is a very useful tool for removing solid waste without having to tip out the whole tray on each occasion, thus allowing you to get a little more mileage from the litter.

When you empty the litter tray, you should wash it out thoroughly with hot water and disinfect it. However, be very careful here, as disinfectants are designed to kill certain bacteria, viruses and fungi, and can also be

A covered litter tray helps to prevent spillage; some types also have odour absorbers or air fresheners in the hood.

dangerous to other organisms. Cats in particular are highly sensitive to certain chemicals found in disinfectants. Some of the most dangerous are those containing phenol (found in TCP and similar disinfectants), cresols (found in Jeyes fluid, Lysol and similar disinfectants) and chloroxylenols (found in Dettol). Other chemicals that you should steer clear of include hexachlorophone, iodine and iodophors. Refer to the disinfectant container for details of the chemicals used, and ask your vet's advice if you are in any doubt.

Whatever disinfectant you choose for cleaning the litter tray, do not be tempted to use a higher-strength solution than is recommended on the label 'just to be sure', as doing this can considerably increase the risks of a low-toxicity product.

Teaching your kitten to use the tray

Kittens are fast learners when it comes to litter training, and must discover how to do so for themselves when very young. In fact, most of any additional work required will usually have been done by the kitten's mother before you bring the kitten home – if she used a litter tray, her kittens will have learned what to do by watching and copying her. As a result, all that you should need to do is to show and then regularly remind the kitten where its new litter tray is over the first few days. If the kitten needs a little encouragement, show it what to do by placing it on the litter tray and, holding its paws, gently scratching and digging the litter – it will soon get the idea.

When you first arrive home with the kitten, lift it on to the tray so that it can relieve itself. If nothing happens at first, repeat the procedure at regular intervals until you have success. If the kitten has an 'accident' elsewhere, put it on to the tray again, along with the tissue or cloth that you have used to mop up urine or any faeces deposited in the wrong place. The smell will help the kitten to associate the tray with the functions that you wish it to perform there.

Clean up the area of the 'accident' thoroughly with a solution of a biological washing powder, rinse it and leave it to dry before you allow the kitten to return there, or it may be attracted to use the spot again. Never 'rub the kitten's nose in it', as this will only make it nervous and more likely to perform in the wrong place. It will also make the kitten fearful of you. (For further information on problems associated with litter training, see page 144.)

To encourage use of the tray, place the kitten on to the litter after feeding and on waking from sleep, as these are the most likely times when it will need to empty its bladder or bowels.

Toileting outdoors

If you intend to allow your kitten to go to the toilet outdoors, you may wish to encourage it to stop using the indoor litter tray and to switch to the soil. (If you keep your kitten indoors at night or any other time, you must of course continue to provide a litter tray inside the house during these periods.) If you have installed a cat flap, you can assist this process by gradually moving the tray closer and closer to the door, at the same time adding some soil to the litter so that the kitten begins to associate soil with toileting.

At first, tip the contents of the litter tray out on to the garden near the kitten's usual exit point, instead of disposing of them, so that again the kitten associates the appropriate smells and substrates, and gets the message that it can use the soil for toileting (however, do not do this if you have dogs or children who could get at the dirty litter). Finally, move the tray so that it is outside the door, leaving it there until the kitten no longer uses it.

Finally, on an important note of hygiene, be sure to cover over any children's sandpits or sand boxes in your garden when they are not in use. If you do not do so, it is highly likely that your kitten – as well as any other cats which happen to be roaming about in the vicinity – will look on them as ideal large litter trays.

CHAPTER NINE

HEALTH CARE

Keeping your kitten fit and healthy does not simply mean taking it to the vet if it becomes ill or is injured. One of your first considerations will be vaccination, but,

A vet will discover a great deal about your kitten's well-being through physical examination.

whether you buy your kitten from a breeder who has completed the kitten's primary-vaccination regime or you obtain it from an owner who has left vaccinations completely up to you, you need to find a vet.

When you first bring your kitten home, it is also wise to go along and register the kitten as a patient and have it checked over by your vet, who may notice something that you have missed in your initial health check (see pages 34–6). In addition, the vet will be able to advise you on diet, vaccinations, worming and health matters in general.

FINDING A VET

Most people use their local veterinary centre for convenience, and are very pleased with the service that it provides. If you live in an urban area, the majority of patients here are likely to be dogs and cats, along with some budgies, hamsters, rabbits and a few exotic pets such as lizards and snakes. A centre of this kind will be well equipped for feline work, and is likely to be knowledgeable about the latest developments in feline medicine. There is also an increasing number of vets in such centres who limit their work solely to cats.

If you live in a rural area, it may be worth looking at all the veterinary centres in your vicinity and finding out whether any have a special interest in cats, as many of the vets working at this type of centre may concentrate on large animals and leave the small-animal or pet work to one person within the practice. You could also ask other cat owners in the area if they can recommend a good 'cat vet'.

If you have a number of choices available in your area, you will need to decide whether you would prefer a large centre with numerous vets and probably (but not always) a more extensive range of specialist equipment for treating small animals; or a smaller practice where you are likely to see the same vet on each visit and so build up more of a relationship with him or her.

Veterinary centres also vary in how much they charge for their services, which may be a consideration, but bear in mind that the cheapest option may not be the best one for your kitten.

VACCINATIONS

A vaccination works by exposing the body's immune system to a harmless quantity of a particular infectious agent. The white blood cells in the body then produce antibodies which attack the infectious agent. By remembering the exact design of these antibodies, the body can mount a rapid and strong immune response if it comes into contact with the disease again, making the cat immune to that virus or bacteria for as long as the vaccination lasts.

A kitten is usually vaccinated at between eight and 10 weeks of age, with a second dose given at 12 weeks. Full protection will not be achieved for seven to 10 days after the second vaccination, so a kitten must not be allowed outdoors, where it could meet other cats, during this period. Your kitten will need annual 'booster' vaccinations to maintain its immunity.

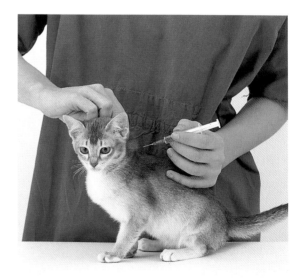

Keeping up to date with a routine vaccination programme is vital to protect your kitten against a number of serious feline infectious diseases (see pages 89–91).

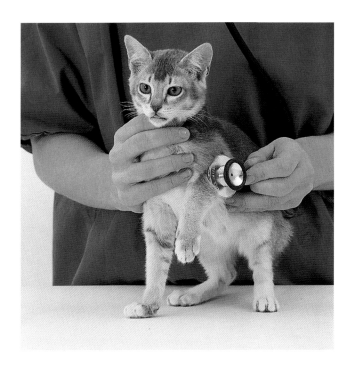

A full veterinary examination of your kitten, which should be carried out soon after you bring the kitten home (see page 61), will involve a number of basic tests, including listening to its heartbeat with the aid of a stethoscope.

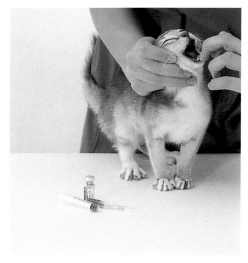

Your kitten's initial check-up is likely to include taking its body temperature rectally with a thermometer; the vet will also do this if at any time the kitten appears to be sick in the future.

Your vet will check inside the kitten's mouth to see that the gums are healthy and that there are no problems with the teeth. Brushing your kitten's teeth regularly will help to prevent problems (see pages 100–1).

If you need to put your kitten into a boarding cattery, make sure that you allow sufficient time for vaccinations. Any good cattery will ask for proof of vaccination, both for your kitten's protection and for that of the other resident cats (see pages 106–8).

Feline diseases

Your kitten will be vulnerable to a number of diseases, although those to which it may be exposed will vary according to where you live (for instance, the rabies virus is found in all continents except Australasia and Antarctica, but the UK is currently free of it). Your kitten's chances of encountering the organisms responsible for disease will depend to some extent on its lifestyle – a kitten which goes outside and regularly meets other cats will be at greater risk than one confined indoors.

Vaccinations are available against the following infectious diseases: feline panleukopaenia infection (also called feline infectious enteritis), feline upper-respiratory-tract disease (caused by one of two viruses: feline herpesvirus type 1 [FHV-1] and feline calicivirus [FCV]), feline chlamydial infection, feline leukaemia virus infection (FeLV) and rabies. The names alone are enough to make you rush to protect your kitten!

A vaccine against feline infectious peritonitis (FIP) has been developed in the USA, but it is rather ineffective and is not yet available in the UK. There is as yet no vaccine against feline immunodeficiency virus (FIV).

Feline panleukopaenia infection This highly infectious disease causes a severe and often fatal gastroenteritis. Any cat may suffer from panleukopaenia, but it mainly affects young kittens. The disease is generally transmitted through direct contact with an infected cat, or through exposure to contaminated objects.

Vaccination provides a high level of long-lasting protection.

Feline upper-respiratory-tract disease The FHV-1 or FCV virus infects the respiratory system, causing the disease commonly called 'cat 'flu'. It is common in places where many cats are kept together, such as at catteries. The disease is not normally life-threatening, but can cause long-term problems such as persistent coughing and 'snuffles'.

The vaccines against cat 'flu may not prevent a cat from becoming infected, but will significantly reduce the severity of the disease.

Feline chlamydial infection This is a particular problem in colonies of cats. Chlamydia is a bacterium which can cause swelling and painful inflammation of the conjunctiva (the membrane around the eye) in a condition known as conjunctivitis. The infection is most prevalent in kittens of five weeks to nine months, and a whole litter may be affected. The disease is generally transmitted by contact with an infected cat.

Vaccination is recommended particularly for cats exposed to environments in which the infection is, or has been in the past, a problem.

Feline leukaemia virus infection This disease is a relatively new discovery, for which vaccines have only been available for a few years. While most cats are able to combat this disease themselves, some 30 per cent of those which come into contact with the virus will become what is called 'persistently affected' and unable to rid their bodies of it. Infection suppresses the immune system, and an infected cat can develop tumours or other diseases associated with its inability to fight off infection. Saliva is the most common source of infection, and the virus is generally transmitted via cat bites or by regular close contact.

The current vaccines against FeLV provide a good level of protection. However, because the virus can take many months before it actually causes disease, an infected cat may appear normal, or simply a little quiet and off-colour. Your vet may therefore suggest carrying out a blood test on your kitten prior to vaccination, to ensure that it is not already infected with the virus.

Rabies The rabies virus affects a cat's central nervous system. In almost all cases it is transmitted by bite, as the virus is present in the saliva of infected animals. A slight change in temperament and excessive licking at the bite-wound area may be succeeded by the so-called 'furious' stage of increasing nervousness, irritability and lack of co-ordination, or the cat may instead progress straight from the initial symptoms to fits, paralysis, coma and death.

In countries where rabies is a potential problem, your kitten should be routinely vaccinated against the virus (your vet will advise you on this); in the UK, vaccines are currently only given to cats which are due to be exported to another country or are entering quarantine.

Feline infectious peritonitis This virus is transmitted through contact with the faeces or saliva of an infected cat, usually before that cat shows symptoms itself. The result of infection will depend on factors such as the cat's age and the state of its immune system.

If the immune system cannot fight off the infection, it will spread around the body in one of two forms – 'wet' FIP (in which symptoms such as abdominal swelling, fever, anaemia and depression develop in just a few weeks), or 'dry' FIP (in which symptoms – associated with the development of inflammatory growths – take longer to appear and include depression, weight loss and fever). Most cats die as a result of infection with FIP.

Feline immunodeficiency virus infection Infection with this disease results in immunosuppression, in which a cat is unable to fight off infections. FIV belongs to a specific group of viruses which includes FeLV (see above) and HIV (the virus responsible for humans AIDS). Transmission is thought to occur mainly through saliva, making cat bites sustained in fights a common cause. About five weeks after infection a cat may be a little off-colour, but may then suffer no further symptoms for months or even years. When symptoms do develop, they generally result from other recurrent infections because FIV has suppressed the cat's normal immune response.

Many of the anti-viral drugs used to combat HIV have been shown to be effective against FIV, but further tests are needed in the long term. FIV infection is diagnosed by a blood test. If a cat is infected, diligent health care and routine vaccinations are especially important. The cat may be kept safely with uninfected ones, provided that they do not fight, but the cats should be fed separately as a precaution.

Does vaccination carry risks?

Some owners worry about the risks associated with vaccination, but these are generally low and severe reactions are very rare. Your kitten may have a small lump at the injection site, or may be quiet and off its food for 24 hours, but will soon recover. However, if you are worried by your kitten's behaviour or health after vaccination, you should contact your vet as soon as possible for advice.

WORMING

All cats are at risk of suffering from intestinal worms. When you obtain your kitten you should ask the breeder, owner or animal welfare society whether worming has been carried out and, if so, what type of wormer was used and when it was last given.

Roundworms and tapeworms commonly infest cats, but, depending on the area in which you live, your kitten may also be vulnerable to other types of worm. Heartworm, for example, is prevalent in warm, humid parts of the USA and Australia. Another parasite, which is usually known as lungworm, is thought to be fairly common in cats in the UK, but is rarely a cause of disease. Ask your vet for specific advice on the worming treatments required to protect your kitten.

Roundworms

These worms have pointed, cream-coloured bodies and can grow up to 15 cm (6 in) long. They are very common in young kittens, which can be infested by ingesting worm eggs present in the faeces of another cat or small rodent, or by eating an infested rodent. A queen can also pass the eggs on to her kittens as they drink her milk. It is best to assume that your kitten has roundworms, and therefore to administer worming doses on a regular basis.

Tapeworms

Tapeworms are flat and white, and consist of numerous individual segments. They are less common than roundworms in kittens, but can be passed on by fleas or picked up by eating infested prey.

Worming products

There are many different wormers available, and you should check with your vet as to which are most appropriate for your kitten. A typical regime is to treat a kitten from four to 16 weeks old for roundworms every two weeks; when the kitten is six months old it will require treatment every two to six months against both roundworms and tapeworms. This regime may vary slightly according to the particular products used and the worm burden where you live – your vet will be able to give you specific advice.

FLEAS

If your kitten has an outdoor lifestyle or mixes regularly with other animals, it is almost certain to come into contact with fleas. The most common type of flea is the well-known cat flea, although hedgehog and rabbit fleas will also tuck into a blood meal on a cat when available.

The ubiquitous cat flea lives mainly in the environment, jumping on to a passing cat to feed. Treating your kitten and cleaning its bedding regularly are vital to prevent infestations.

Any fleas that are brought in by your kitten will also infest your home. This is because, although adult fleas live and feed on a cat, the females lay eggs which fall off into carpets or bedding. These first develop into larvae and then into pupae, which can lie dormant until a suitable meal (animal or person) comes along.

Flea larvae favour warm, moist environments, the ideal place being at the bottom of the carpet pile in a centrally heated house. They feed on debris in the carpet – especially the faeces from adult fleas which fall from the kitten along with the eggs. This is a very clever ploy for survival which ensures that you can have fleas in your home all year round, not just in the summer months when they are more common outdoors.

Checking for fleas

Even if your kitten has an infestation of fleas you may not be able to see them, as they can scuttle through the fur at great speed. However, you can easily check your kitten for fleas by brushing its coat on to a piece of damp white blotting paper. Any flea faeces – consisting mainly of digested blood – will show up as black dots surrounded by pink on the white paper, as the blood begins to dissolve.

Some cats do not scratch or show any reaction to the presence of fleas; others develop an allergy to flea saliva, and may groom excessively and develop skin disease. Some kittens rescued from poor environments have heavy flea burdens which can actually cause anaemia (a lack of red blood cells).

Treating your kitten

There are many flea products now available, including sprays, foams, shampoos, powders, spot-on products (one drop is put on the skin at the back of the neck about once a month), tablets, flea collars and even strange ultrasonic devices said to repel fleas.

Sprays are quick and easy to apply, but some cats dislike the sound and feel of them. As an alternative, foams (similar to hair mousses) and other medications may be brushed or stroked into the coat. Shampoos and powders have limited effectiveness because they only work for a short while after application; similarly, flea collars may not work well enough to cope with an environment containing great numbers of fleas.

Ask your vet for advice on which products to choose: this is very important, as certain products must not be used on young kittens. Always read the label and follow dosage instructions carefully, as some flea products can cause problems if used too frequently or in too great a quantity. Do not mix different products unless on the advice of your vet, as you could overdose your kitten.

Treating the environment

Simply treating your kitten for fleas will not solve the problem – you must also tackle them in the environment and on any other animals in the house. Remember, too, that fleas are likely to be brought in subsequently by animals which have regular access outdoors, so it really is a constant battle.

Various products are available to tackle fleas in the home. Some are insecticides and kill on contact; others contain chemicals to inhibit the growth of fleas. Alternatively, if you can interrupt the lifecycle you will prevent new fleas from emerging, and several products aim to do this (for example, one product is given to a cat in its food, and renders flea eggs on the cat incapable of hatching).

Another recently available option is borate powder: this is applied to the whole house by professional operators, and will dry out eggs and larvae in the carpets, flooring and upholstery for a year. This can be expensive, but is much less time-consuming than other methods and is also non-toxic to all inhabitants of the house (except the fleas!). Ask your vet about the treatments available where you live, and for advice on which will be best for you.

Whichever product you use, you will need to treat all areas within the house to which your kitten has access. Take special notice of areas in which the kitten lies, or where it jumps down from a chair or bed, as eggs and larvae are most likely to fall off here. Move pieces of furniture and cushions to treat the areas underneath and behind them, as well as the cracks in wooden floors.

You should also wash your kitten's bedding regularly at a high temperature. When you vacuum the house, throw away the dust bag afterwards as it is likely to contain eggs and larvae which will hatch in it and re-infest the house.

OTHER PARASITES

If your kitten goes outdoors, it may also come into contact with the following parasites. If you are not confident about removing a tick using the method described, or if you are unsure of the identity of a parasite, always take your kitten to the vet for diagnosis and advice on treatment.

Ticks

Ticks are leathery creatures that are visible to the naked eye but become most obvious when their bodies enlarge after feeding. They spend most of their lives in the environment, only visiting cats or other animals to feed for a few days during spring and autumn. Your kitten may pick up ticks by brushing against plants infested with them. Certain ticks can spread serious infections, such as Lyme disease, and may cause skin irritation or even anaemia in a heavy infestation.

To remove a tick, dab it with cotton wool soaked in an appropriate insecticide (ask your vet's advice on this). Leave it for a few minutes to die, then use a pair of tweezers to grasp the tick, rotate it and pull it from the skin. Do this very carefully or you may leave the tick's head embedded in your kitten's skin, which could cause an infection.

Lice

Lice are wingless insects that are spread between cats either through close physical contact, or by sharing bedding and/or grooming tools. They are visible to the naked eye but a magnifying glass will help you to identify them and their eggs, or nits, which will be attached to individual hairs. If your kitten has lice, there may be a 'mousey' smell to the coat and/or signs of skin irritation.

Routine insecticidal treatments used to kill fleas (see above) will kill any lice on your kitten.

Mites

Mites are tiny creatures related to spiders, and various types may affect your kitten (ask your vet's advice on those likely to be a problem in your area). One common example is the ear mite, which spends its life inside an animal's external ear canal; this causes irritation and an excessive production of dark brown wax. Ear mites are passed on by direct contact between cats.

If your kitten is showing signs of ear irritation – such as shaking or scratching its head – take it to your vet, who will prescribe medication to kill the mites and relieve the irritation.

POISONS

Cats are far more fastidious in their eating habits than scavenging dogs, but there are several ways in which a poison can get into a cat's system, besides being eaten. A cat may actually ingest a poison in its efforts to get rid of it: for example, by licking and trying to groom away a toxic substance contaminating the coat; another route of poisoning is by eating prey – usually rodents – which have themselves been poisoned. Some toxins can even be absorbed through the skin, especially the paws: for example, if a cat has walked through a poison such as creosote (wood preserver).

Although cats are poisoned less frequently than dogs, they may not be able to deal with the poison in their bodies as well as their canine cousins because they are small and lack certain enzymes in their bodies which would help to render the toxin harmless.

If you suspect poisoning

There are many signs of poisoning, depending on the actual poison and on the amount taken into the body. Signs can range from vomiting or diarrhoea to neurological indications such as lack of co-ordination or depression. Your kitten's breathing pattern may also change, or it may start drinking water excessively.

If you think that your kitten may have been poisoned, go to your vet immediately. Take the suspected poison – or a note of what was on the label – with you, as identification may make treatment both more rapid and more effective.

If you suspect that your kitten has been licking something from its coat, wrap the kitten in a towel to prevent further ingestion of the poison (this method is also useful for restraint if the kitten is being aggressive or difficult to control). Remove a flea collar if worn (cats are very sensitive to chemicals, and there could possibly be an interaction between those in the collar and a chemical contaminating the skin).

If a contamination of the coat is obvious, very carefully cut away the affected fur before washing the kitten in warm, soapy water (keeping its head above water). It is important to try to remove most of the poison before washing, as the washing process can sometimes enhance a poison's absorption through the skin.

Do not try to make your kitten sick, but if it is vomiting spontaneously note anything unusual about the vomit so that you can inform your vet (for example, a blue colour may indicate consumption of slug pellets or rodent killer). If your kitten will drink, offer milk or water to help dilute the poison and wash through the toxins.

GROOMING

A shiny cat moving gracefully in that dignified manner unique to the feline species is one of nature's wonders. Both wild and domestic cats have some of the most beautiful coats in the animal kingdom, and you can help to keep your kitten's coat in tip-top condition by providing a good diet, proper health care and regular grooming.

A soft toothbrush will be very useful for gently brushing your kitten's face and the sensitive area around its eyes.

Whatever type of kitten you have, regular grooming is not only necessary for coat health but will also enable you to examine the kitten in detail on a frequent basis. You can check for the presence of fleas and other parasites such as ticks or lice, and will feel any unusual lumps and bumps that should be checked by your vet.

As with any sort of handling and routine, the younger your kitten is when you start grooming, the more quickly it will accept the procedure. Accustom the kitten to having its coat brushed, its ears and eyes checked, and its claws trimmed. You may even wish to clean your kitten's teeth (see pages 100–1), in which case you need to start as soon as possible.

It is no good deciding that you want to give a semi-grown cat its first grooming session because its coat is looking very matted, and then to expect it to sit there and accept the pulling and cutting without complaint. If you groom regularly the need for drastic action will be less, and your kitten may even enjoy these sessions if they cause no discomfort. You will then avoid the surprisingly common situation in which an owner has to take a fractious cat to the vet for a general anaesthetic simply to have its matted and dirty coat shorn off. Start early, kindly and firmly, and you may both enjoy the experience and form closer bonds because of it.

Grooming equipment

The extent of your grooming kit will vary according to the type of kitten that you own. For instance, if you have a Persian with a long coat and thick undercoat you will need a number of tools; if you have a short-coated kitten which goes outdoors and looks after itself to a great extent, you will really need very little in the way of grooming equipment to keep its coat in optimum condition.

Many cats – and owners – enjoy the grooming process, and this is an ideal time to strengthen the bond with your kitten. All the members of the family should be shown how to groom and encouraged to take their turn. Most cats are easy to handle during grooming, particularly if they become accustomed to the routine from an early age.

A metal comb is useful for removing loose hair, but never attempt to 'drag' it through the coat as you will hurt your cat – instead, remove tangles gently.

Longhairs and semi-longhairs need particular attention in areas that tend to be prone to matting, such as under the belly and around the tail area.

A cat's tail is very sensitive, so brush or comb the hair here very gently. Hold your kitten gently but firmly – never try to restrain it forcibly.

Finish off the grooming session by gently wiping around your kitten's eyes with cotton wool dipped in clean water (use a new piece for each eye).

For a long-haired kitten you will need several types of brush: one with wider teeth to remove any tangles gently from the coat, and perhaps another, finer wire-and-bristle brush, or a comb, to get into the detail of the undercoat. In addition, a fine-toothed comb (also known as a 'flea' comb) may be very useful. If you do need to cut out a tangle, use scissors with blunt (rounded) ends to avoid any chance of injuring your kitten should it move unexpectedly. A toothbrush is ideal for brushing the hair around the ears and eyes.

For a short-haired kitten, a bristle brush is ideal for removing dirt and loose hairs. A chamois leather, velvet mitt or piece of silk, used after brushing, will bring a shine to the coat.

The soft, sparse coat of the Devon and Cornish Rexes (see page 27) may need more gentle attention with a soft-bristled brush.

When and how to groom

Ideally, and whatever its type of coat, you should give your kitten a thorough groom at least once a week, with an additional tidy-up as necessary. Always start with the least sensitive parts of the kitten's body (such as its back), and finish with the more sensitive areas (such as under its tail and between the hindlegs).

With a long-haired kitten, check the fur under the base of the tail and at the backs of the hindlegs to ensure that it has not become soiled (particularly if your kitten has suffered from a bout of diarrhoea); if so, gently remove any soiling with dampened cotton wool. You must also check the hair between the toes, as this can become choked with damp litter and contents from the litter tray.

Almost all cats moult or shed hair in the spring – and to some extent in the autumn – and so you may need to groom your kitten more frequently during this period. This will help to remove excess hair and prevent it from being ingested and forming hair balls in the stomach. Grooming it out will also help to prevent the spread of hair around your house!

Eyes Cats with very flat faces may have constantly moist eyes because the fluid cannot drain properly through the tear duct, causing tear staining on the fur at the inner corners of the eyes. Gently wipe this away with cotton wool dampened with clean water or a little baby oil. Use a separate piece of cotton wool for each eye and dry with cotton wool or a tissue, making sure that you do not touch the sensitive eyeball.

If your kitten needs eye drops, you must administer them very carefully. Keep the kitten's head still, and do not position the bottle too close to the eye in case the kitten moves suddenly.

Ears If you feel that you should clean your kitten's ears because they look a little grubby inside, take great care. Most vets would advise you not to tamper with the ears at all, as the tissues lining the ear canals are very delicate and easily damaged. However, if you do feel that it is necessary to clean your kitten's ears, use cotton wool moistened with baby oil and just wipe the outer part of the ears with a very light motion. NEVER poke the cotton wool into the inner ears.

If your kitten suffers from an infestation of ear mites (see pages 94–5), your vet is likely to prescribe ear drops to kill the mites and relieve the irritation. Holding the kitten's head and ear, gently administer the drops and then massage around the outside of the base of the ear to spread the liquid evenly and thoroughly.

A good pair of 'guillotine' clippers, specifically designed for the purpose, will make claw trimming easy. An indoor cat in particular may need its claws attended to regularly, as it will not wear them down naturally as an outdoor cat will do.

If there are large deposits of wax in the ears, or the ears look red, take your kitten for a check-up with your vet in case it is suffering from ear mites or an infection.

Claws If your kitten does not go outside and wear down its claws naturally through climbing trees and other activities, you may like to invest in a pair of good-quality 'guillotine' clippers to clip the claws neatly and safely as necessary. If left untrimmed over a long period,

(Above) Tooth-brushing is a process that needs to be carried out gradually and gently. At first, simply allow your kitten to become used to the brush.

(Left) Always brush gently, using special feline toothpaste.

claws can actually grow around into the footpads, causing great discomfort. Look carefully at each of your kitten's claws and be sure to clip below the little blood vessel in the claw (this is visible as a thin red line which gradually disappears). Work quickly and calmly so that your kitten does not become agitated.

Teeth A regular check in and around your kitten's mouth will reveal any lurking problems, from sore gums or a build-up of tartar on the teeth to broken teeth or lumps which should not be there. There are now kits available containing brushes or little fabric pads designed to slip on to a finger to clean a cat's teeth, along with feline toothpastes (these are similar to human toothpastes, but are more palatable to cats and do not foam) and cleaners. Just as human teeth benefit from brushing to prevent the build-up of tartar, a regular clean will do the same for your kitten's teeth.

Your kitten will lose most of its milk (baby) teeth by the age of about five months, so do not panic if you see a tiny tooth coming out. Check that this has not been caused by an injury of any kind and that the mouth looks normal, and then don't worry – another tooth will soon come through in its place.

GIVING YOUR KITTEN MEDICINE

If your kitten has to take medication for any reason – be it a regular worming dose or a drug prescribed by your vet – you need to know how best to get the medicine into the kitten so that it receives the correct dose. Kittens are very small and can easily be overdosed – they are also very wriggly and capable of spitting out most of what has been put in their mouths.

You must be accurate in your dosing, so weigh your kitten and check the dose that you need to give (if your vet has not already done so for you). Cut up large tablets or measure out powder accurately. Check whether the medicine needs to be given on an empty stomach or with food, as this can affect how efficiently it works, and also at what time of day you should administer it.

Always complete a course of treatment – never alter the medicine dosage or stop it unless your vet tells you to do so. If you are worried about your kitten's lack of response – or seemingly strange response – to a medicine, consult your vet.

Giving a medicine with food

Provided that it is acceptable to give the medication with your kitten's food (always check this with your vet first), you can hide small tablets in a little tasty food such as cheese, butter or a piece of meat, or crush them and mix them with the kitten's usual food. Powders and syrups may also be given in this way.

However, kittens are very adept at detecting 'doctored' food, and, if your kitten refuses to eat it, you will have to try the conventional method of administering a tablet by mouth (see below). Similarly, if you have several cats, or any other animals which may eat the food, you will need to feed the kitten alone, or to try alternative tactics. If the kitten only eats a part of the food, it may also be quite difficult to gauge how much of the medicine has gone down.

Giving a tablet

If you really want to be sure that your kitten has taken all the medication required, you may need to give it by mouth. In this case, having an assistant to restrain the kitten for you will make the process much easier (when the kitten is small you may be able to manage alone, but kittens can be extremely wriggly and the following two-person method works well as they grow and become less easy to control). If no assistant is available, you can restrain the kitten if necessary by wrapping its body firmly in a large towel.

With your kitten properly restrained by a helper, and the tablet ready in your fingers, gently open the kitten's mouth.

1 Sit the kitten on a table, in front of and facing away from your helper, and then ask him or her to clasp their palms around its chest. The kitten is very likely to attempt to prevent you from dosing it by using its front paws, so your helper should hold its forelegs securely between their third and fourth fingers, and use their arm and upper body to hold the kitten firmly to their side so that it cannot wriggle away.

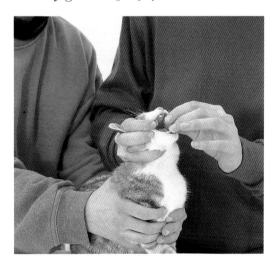

Drop the tablet as far back into the mouth as possible, on the centre of the tongue, so that the kitten cannot spit it out.

2 Stand at the side or in front of the kitten. Place the palm of your hand over the kitten's head with your thumb and third finger on either side of the angle of the jaw, so that you are in effect holding the upper jaw and head.

3 Take the tablet between the thumb and second finger of your other hand, and place your fore-finger on the lower teeth at the front of the mouth.

4 Tilt back the kitten's head and press on the corners of the mouth to ease it open. Gently but firmly, press down on the lower jaw and drop the tablet as far back into the throat as possible so that the kitten cannot spit it out again.

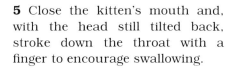

Still holding the kitten's head tilting upwards, gently stroke down the throat with a finger: this will encourage swallowing.

5 Close the kitten's mouth and, with the head still tilted back, stroke down the throat with a finger to encourage swallowing.

Pill dispensers or 'guns' These simple devices – available from many veterinary centres – can make the whole process of giving tablets easier and reduce the chances of having a finger bitten by a particularly fractious feline. You will have to discover the best method for giving tablets to your kitten – some are easy and calm, and some fight to the bitter end!

Administering a liquid

If you need to give a liquid medicine, restrain your kitten (as described on the opposite page) and use a syringe to introduce the medication. To do this, gently push the nozzle of the syringe between the teeth at the side of the kitten's mouth and then squeeze in the fluid very slowly – aiming diagonally across the mouth rather than down the throat – so that it has a chance to swallow.

A pill dispenser, or 'gun', can make giving a tablet easier – this may be useful if your kitten dislikes the procedure.

Giving eye drops or ointment

If you need to treat your kitten's eye with drops or ointment, first ensure that the eye is clean by gently removing any discharge with dampened cotton wool. Restrain the kitten (see page 102) and open the upper eyelid with the thumb and finger of one hand. Holding the dropper or tube slightly away from the eye in case your kitten should move suddenly, administer the drops or ointment directly into the eye.

Giving ear drops

To give ear drops, restrain your kitten (see page 102), turn its head to one side and then drop in the medicine. Gently massage the outside of the ear to spread the medication around the whole area.

COPING WITH AN EMERGENCY

If your kitten suddenly becomes ill, collapses or is involved in a road-traffic accident, you will need to contact your vet as soon as possible. Always keep the telephone number handy with that of your own doctor, and make sure that everyone in the household knows where it is.

If you make your emergency call at night, follow up the message on the answerphone or wait to be transferred to the vet on call. Veterinary centres have a duty to provide 24-hour cover for the animals in their care, so you will always be able to contact a vet in a genuine emergency. Try not to panic, as you will be much better able to reassure your kitten if you remain calm yourself. If the kitten is in imminent danger, such as on a road, gently place it on a towel or blanket and move it to safety.

In an emergency your vet will usually ask you to bring the kitten into the veterinary centre, so that he or she has access to the full range of equipment. If you can put your kitten in its carrier, do so; if not, wrap it in a blanket and hold it firmly but gently so that it cannot try to escape.

INSURING YOUR KITTEN

For an annual premium, many insurance companies in the UK will provide cover for veterinary expenses incurred with your kitten, as well as paying boarding-cattery fees if you are ill, cancellation costs if your kitten needs surgery just before you were due to go on holiday, or the cost of the kitten following loss or death after an accident or illness.

If you buy a pedigree kitten it may come with cover for the first few weeks, and the company will then contact you to ask whether you wish to continue the insurance for the year. This is sensible, as the first year is the time when accidents often happen, and the veterinary fees for treating your kitten after a car accident or a bad fall could be high.

If you live outside the UK, consult your vet or an insurance company to find out whether a similar type of cover for pets is available in your country and, if so, what the costs would be for your kitten.

Chapter Ten

GOING ON HOLIDAY

Many owners do not fully enjoy their holidays because they cannot help worrying about the welfare of their cats or kittens while they are away. However, with a little organization and research you should find a good solution and will be able to go for a well-deserved rest, knowing that your kitten is in good hands.

LEAVING YOUR KITTEN WITH A NEIGHBOUR

Leaving a young kitten alone in the house, with a neighbour coming in to feed and check on it – even just for two or three days – is not a very good idea, no matter how dependable the neighbour. Kittens get up to all sorts of mischief, especially if they are bored, so if you could arrange for a friend to stay in your house and provide more constant care, this would be preferable to someone popping in once or even twice a day.

If you do choose the neighbour option, remember that while you are away your kitten should not be allowed outdoors, in case it feels confused and wanders off. Caring for another person's pet is a great responsibility, and even a temporary disappearance by your kitten would be very upsetting both for you and for the person left in charge. Instead, provide an indoor litter tray for the kitten to use and be sure to leave full instructions regarding food, water, play, medications and so on for your carer to follow.

When your kitten is a little older, you may be able to trust its care to a neighbour who will visit several times a day to put down fresh food and give it some attention. You will have to decide whether to let the kitten out over this period or to keep it in where you know it will be safe. This very much depends on the kitten – for instance, an older kitten or cat which is used to being alone (and which is likely to sleep most of the day away) will probably be quite safe for a day or two. The younger the cat, the more advisable it is to keep it indoors for the short period you are going to be away.

Before you leave, give the person looking after your kitten details of where to contact you in an emergency, as well as the address and telephone number of your veterinary centre. Drawing a map of how to get to the centre will be helpful if the person is not familiar with the area. It is also a good idea to inform your vet that you will be away.

CAT SITTERS

Another option is to pay for the services of a house or cat sitter. A house sitter will actually stay in your home to look after your kitten and possessions; a cat sitter will visit once or twice a day to tend to the kitten. Provided that the sitter is reliable, and that you will not be away for a very lengthy period (this is important if you have a young kitten, and are using the cat-sitter option, rather than a resident house sitter), this can work very well. If you have a number of animals, it may also be the most cost-effective solution.

If house or cat sitters are available in your area, check that they have good references and plenty of experience, and, if possible, talk to other cat owners who have used them on previous occasions.

CHOOSING A BOARDING CATTERY

If you are going away for more than a few days and do not know of someone to 'cat sit', the best way to ensure your kitten's health and safety is to choose a good boarding cattery. Sadly, there are many poorly run catteries, so what are the criteria for a good one?

You obviously need to know that your kitten will be safe and properly fed, but you also want a cattery to be run by staff who will spend time with the kitten and make it feel at home – in other words, to care for it as you do. The premises must also be clean and hygienic. Below are some pointers to help you choose a cattery at which you can leave your kitten with confidence.

Minimizing infections

Despite recent advances in our understanding and knowledge of cats, and of the diseases from which they suffer, many catteries are still run by apparently well-meaning people who offer living conditions hazardous to the cat. High on this list are catteries offering communal runs or exercise areas, or in which contact between cats in their enclosures is possible.

Nowadays, more cats are being exposed to feline chlamydial infection, FeLV, rabies (outside the UK) and FIV, to name just a few diseases (see pages 89–91). It is therefore imperative that catteries are built to specifications which preclude any form of contact between the boarders, while still allowing them the pleasure of viewing one another and communicating across barriers. These barriers should be either 50-cm (20-in) gaps or full-height solid partitions – so-called 'sneeze barriers' – between runs, to prevent airborne transmission of infectious diseases. Each cat (or cats from the same household) should be provided with a separate unit, containing both a sleeping area and an outdoor run, and any cattery housing all cats indoors with a shared air supply should be avoided. There should also be isolation facilities available for sick cats.

Choosing a good boarding cattery means that both you and your kitten will enjoy the holiday. Taking your kitten's bed, bowls and some favourite toys will make it feel at home.

The cattery should insist that your kitten has been fully vaccinated against feline panleukopaenia infection and cat 'flu, and that the vaccinations – whether primary or 'booster' injections – have been carried out far enough in advance to allow maximum protection (see page 87). This should be a fundamental requirement for any cattery. Many cats carry latent health problems which may manifest themselves under stress and can be transmitted to other cats, and a stay in a cattery – especially a poorly run one – can be just such a trigger.

Clean, pleasant premises

If the cattery proprietor will not give you a tour, look elsewhere. The owner of a good cattery will be pleased to let you see how it is run and where your kitten will be kept. It is better to search further afield, and to be prepared for a slightly longer journey to reach the cattery, than to subject your kitten to a period of privation in a poor establishment.

Look for clean, well-kept premises in tidy, well-tended surroundings. The cattery buildings should be well maintained, and the enclosures and their concrete bases free of algae stains. The accommodation for each cat should include a comfortable sleeping and an open-air exercise area of reasonable size.

Many catteries make a lot of effort to ensure not only that cats in their care are kept cleanly and safely, but that they have an interesting view. For instance, the cattery may be in sight of the owner's house so that the occupants can watch people coming and going, or may be planted with flowers which attract butterflies, providing something to watch.

The cats should look contented, and there should be no smell, either of faeces and urine or of strong disinfectant used to disguise inadequate cleaning. Water bowls should be clean and filled with fresh water; food bowls should also be clean or disposable, and the food provided fresh and suitable to each individual.

Look at the state of the litter trays – are they clean and sufficiently large, and what type of litter is used? Check the provision of heating or a cooling system – is it individually controlled for each unit, and is there an extra charge for electricity? Some cats – depending on their age, coat and what they are used to at home – feel the cold much more than others, and their special needs should be met.

Caring proprietors

A good guide to assessing the caring nature of a proprietor is whether he or she asks you about your kitten's history (particularly its medical history) and checks that its vaccinations are up to date. You should also find out whether the cattery would be prepared to continue with any ongoing medication prescribed for the kitten by your vet. The proprietor should ask about your kitten's diet, its likes and dislikes, and any foibles such as not liking to be picked up by strangers.

Find out what would happen if your kitten were unwell, or if you were unable to collect it on the agreed date. When you leave your kitten at a cattery, be sure that the owner knows how to contact you in an emergency, and has the details of your usual veterinary centre.

Cattery requirements

In the UK, details of requirements for boarding catteries are given in the Model Licence Conditions and Guidelines, which is published by the Chartered Institute of Environmental Health. An updated version of this document – compiled with the help of the Feline Advisory Bureau, or FAB (see page 158 for contact details) – was produced in 1996. FAB publishes a list of approved catteries which meet its stringent requirements for accommodation construction and cat management. Often these catteries have been built to very rigorous standards, the owners have attended a course of boarding-cattery management, and the cattery has undergone a detailed inspection. FAB also provides a subsidiary list of catteries which fall just below these very rigorous standards, but which are still excellent.

If you live outside the UK, find out from your veterinary centre whether a similar scheme is in operation, or ask for recommendations of good boarding catteries in your area.

CHAPTER ELEVEN

CAT BEHAVIOUR

Cats are an exception among all our domesticated animals in that they are obligate predators and have retained many of their wild outdoor instincts. Some owners become distressed by the hunting activity of their cats – which will continue regardless of whether plenty of food is provided for them at home – but this is entirely natural behaviour. Indeed, it is this aspect of the feline character, combined with its very loving nature, that makes cats such intriguing and rewarding companions.

The body shape and general appearance of today's domestic Shorthair has not changed significantly from that of its ancestor, the African wild cat (see below and page 110).

With the help of new DNA technology, scientists have now proved beyond doubt that the domestic cat is the true descendant of just one species, Felis sylvestris lybica, *or the African wild cat. This animal, with its strong, agile physique and beautifully marked coat, is fairly tolerant of human beings and can still be found living in and around villages in various parts of Africa, scavenging for food as well as hunting.*

To understand our relationship with the cat today, it is first necessary to look back at how that relationship evolved and has developed over thousands of years and in different parts of the world.

THE HISTORY OF MAN AND CAT

Evidence has been found of cats living in association with humans from about 1500 BC in Ancient Egypt, and archaeological studies in the region point to the African wild cat (*Felis sylvestris lybica*) as the main ancestor of our modern pet cat. Indeed, recent studies in South Africa have been unable to distinguish the DNA of the domestic cat from that of the African wild cat, while the European wild cat – which is often assumed to have contributed to the pet cat's development – is clearly distinguishable from both.

The implication is that the pet cat is still genetically almost identical to the African wild cat. To explain this, the local population of the African wild cat in the Nile Delta must have become less reactive to the usually threatening presence and activity of man, enabling it to remain close to human settlements. African wild cats with this decreased sensitivity would then have been able to exploit the resources of higher concentrations of rodents living around man's grain stores, edible waste in dumps and better shelter. They would have bred with much-improved chances of success

The relationship between man and cat is an ancient one, and cats have exploited the presence of humans to the full in their search for food and shelter.

and, because small cats can reproduce relatively frequently (with two or even three litters per year), populations of 'friendly' African wild cats living alongside humans would have developed very quickly in Ancient Egypt.

The beginnings of domestication

The kittens of these wild cats would soon have had physical contact with people, being taken into their homes for care and coming to view them as substitute parents. Their infantile dependency would have been maintained by early handling and perhaps feeding during the 'sensitive' period of socialization from two to seven/eight weeks (see pages 43–4). Indeed, it is remarkable that in and around the human den in this more urban habitat, the cat has become much more sociable with its own kind and with other species – such as humans and dogs – in comparison with its previous highly territorial behaviour in the wild.

This localized decreased sensitivity in the reactivity of the African wild cat perhaps explains why a close companion-animal relationship became uniquely established between this species and man, yet without affecting the cat's predatory behaviour (see pages 113–16), which is dictated by other parts of its brain.

Additional evidence of this is that feral kittens, born to free-living queens anywhere in the world, can be easily tamed and will become friendly adult pet cats for life if they are handled to establish the substitute-parent relationship and are 'stress-immunized' to human activity within the 'sensitive' socialization period. Kittens of other species of small cat – such as the European wild cat – even if they are initially infantile and accepting of human contact up to the age of weaning, then cease to regard their human surrogates as parental figures. They become increasingly reactive to approach and socially independent as they reach sexual maturity, and cannot be kept as friendly, cuddly pets at all.

Further developments

Cats were latecomers on the domestic scene compared with dogs and other animals domesticated for food purposes such as sheep, chickens and ducks. These are all known to have been living with humans in the Mesolithic Age, at least 8000 to 10,000 years earlier than when the first cats are recorded as living in association with man.

The domestic cat, while giving great affection and loyalty to its owner, still retains much of the independence of spirit and natural hunting instincts of an animal living in the wild.

However, once this unique relationship had begun, there is great evidence of cats being kept as companions in an area radiating out from Ancient Egypt via known trade routes throughout the world. For example, a terracotta head of a cat and a fresco depicting the cat dating from 1500–1100 BC (the late Minoan period) have been discovered in Crete, a nearby civilization with which the maritime Egyptians are most likely to have traded. By 500 BC the cat appears to have become a regular feature of folklore and civilized life in mainland Greece and elsewhere in southern Europe.

The cat was also depicted in Roman religion – in many art forms – at the feet of Diana, Goddess of Light. Pliny mentioned the hunting of the cat in his *Natural History*, written in AD 77, and, in the third century, Palladius recommended using cats to catch moles. It is probable that cats were still kept and transported during this period

(Left) Cats were revered as sacred creatures in Ancient Egypt, and thousands of them were mummified and placed in lavishly decorated sarcophagi.

(Above) A representation of the cat-headed fertility goddess Bast. A temple at Bubastis was devoted to her, with a yearly festival held in her honour.

(Above and left) Cats featured regularly in the paintings of the Ancient Egyptians.

(predominantly to keep down rats and mice on board ship, and then in newly settled towns around the world), and that they were sold and bartered for the same purpose.

The other indigenous small wild cats around the world, such as the European wild cat, were – and still are – very shy and fearful of humans, compared with the mutated African wild cats brought by traders. By virtue of their innate adaptability to new environments and their continuing tolerance of humans, the immigrant cats quickly and firmly established themselves in and around their settlements. They then out-competed their wild relatives, and their populations expanded along with man's urbanization of the countryside. Many of these cats then adopted more of a free-living lifestyle, being at least partially dependent on their own hunting skills and not solely on man's direct or indirect provision of food.

The pet cat

The cat's entry to our homes as a pet – as opposed to living 'free' around our farms and towns – became established in Europe perhaps over 2000 years after it had done so in the Ancient Egyptians' homes. In more recent times this has paved the way for a much greater selection of the cat for human standards of beauty, in breeds determined solely by their physical appearance at cat shows. Only about 10 per cent of pet cats are of recognized breeds, usually defined by the length and colour of their coats and their physical shape; the vast majority of our pets are non-pedigree cats and come in a huge variety of colours.

The African wild cat that we now recognize as 'domestic' has been subjected to far less selective breeding for type (and none for task) than our pet dogs, and over a much shorter time-scale. Unlike the domestic dog when compared with its ancestor, the wolf, the cat's physical and behavioural characteristics are virtually unchanged from those of its wild ancestor. For example, most cats naturally still carry out the sequence of predatory behaviour: stalking, chasing, catching and killing their prey of birds and small rodents, while few types of domestic dog can complete such a hunting sequence to feed themselves.

PREDATORY BEHAVIOUR

The ultimate sheltered biological niche in the world must be as a pet in a human's den. It is warm in winter, cool in summer, draught-proof and full of comfortable resting places, not to mention the food which miraculously appears to replenish empty dishes. So it is often a source of great frustration for owners of valuable pedigree and non-pedigree cats alike that our pampered pets still hunt, especially during the springtime. However, undoing 13 million years of perfected evolutionary process is impossible, and, apart from keeping your kitten indoors, you can do little to prevent it from hunting.

Although the cat uses its teeth and its claws in hunting, predatory attacks tend to be silent and straightforward, and composed of a fairly rigid sequence of behaviour: 'eye-stalk-pounce-grasp-bite-kill'. The object is not to communicate with prey but to capture, kill and eat it, so it is futile for a mouse, for example, to try to appease a cat by rolling on its back to avoid being eaten.

Why do pet cats need to kill?

Few owners complain when their cats catch an occasional mouse or kill a rat, but the first damp-feathered songbird fledgelings brought in during the spring are very upsetting. But why should a well-fed cat need to kill anything at all?

Not all the prey killed by a cat is required for food, but mice and birds are used for the purposes of practice for the hunter. Research has shown that prey hunting and killing occur independently of hunger in the cat, so your kitten – given the opportunity – will not be able to help hunting, and will simply be performing its natural behaviour.

Why do cats play with their victims?

Many owners are distressed by the way that cats appear to play with their prey, apparently torturing it to death rather than ending its days quickly with a rapid, fatal bite to the nape of the neck.

When such play is prolonged, it can be indicative of an incomplete learning programme when the cat was young – particularly in one brought up indoors by a mother who did not bring home half-dead mice on which her kittens could practise and develop their killing skills. Hence the cat will 'bat' and play with its victim only as far as it used to bat and play with toys, its littermates and its mother's tail when it was a kitten exploring the capacity of its physical abilities.

The cat may also use the half-dead prey to practise its hunting abilities for the next occasion, safe in the knowledge that this particular victim has already been taken and can be killed and consumed at any time. Another factor is that the well-fed pet has never had to learn to kill its prey quickly to relieve great hunger. A cat may see its owner as a friend or perhaps even as a kitten in the shared den, and may bring its quarry in for the owner to play with and learn how to kill, or to ensure that he or she maintains the ability to do so.

When you are the prey!

A cat possesses innate hunting skills, but it cannot become an efficient predator and hunt successfully without refining these skills. It must frequently exercise its reflexes and practise its agility, co-ordination of senses and muscular control in play with objects or with anyone it can persuade to play the role of 'victim', such as another friendly cat, the family dog or its owner! Indeed, all play in adult cats is now regarded primarily as hunting practice for the predator.

As with true predatory behaviour, the cat seldom makes any sound during these play 'attacks'. Young cats are most likely to attack their owners in this way as they seek to develop into expert predators, but mature cats also play like this. Such attacks are almost invariably triggered by a movement of the 'victim', and some cats learn to lie in wait to ambush their owners from a favourite vantage point behind a door or chair as they pass. A 'victim' may be stalked and pounced on in this way, but the force of the final 'killing' bite – although often painful – is usually inhibited and the claws may be kept retracted.

To avoid injury, carry small toys with you around the house, or leave them lying near known sites of attack to throw ahead as you pass or to divert your kitten's attention if it becomes over-excited when playing with other toys. Never respond to being pounced on with a counter-attack of hitting or pushing your kitten away, as this may be interpreted as reciprocal play. If your kitten feels threatened by such reactions it may run away and give you the impression that your response has reformed its behaviour, or may fight back in self-defence. Either way, the problem of attacking you will then become much worse and harder to treat, because the kitten will be more strongly motivated in future through the added element of threat.

The importance of play

If your kitten lives indoors, it is essential that you play with it frequently and provide outlets for its predatory behaviour every day by offering moving safe targets to stalk, chase and pounce on, even if the final 'kill' is restricted to inanimate toys. A playful kitten needs to be played with, using safe toys moved about erratically to elicit and sustain interest. This is especially important if your kitten has learned to focus its predatory practice behaviour (play) on you, or is forced to do so by being kept in an unchanging environment without stimulating prey substitutes.

Cats are designed to survive on about 10 mouse-size rodents per day – derived from, say, 30 hunting attempts – so 30 is perhaps the minimum number of short predatory 'play' sessions that might benefit an indoor cat. Do invest the necessary time and effort to fulfil these, especially if your kitten is to spend its life predominantly or totally indoors.

Time spent playing not only helps to strengthen the bond between kitten and owner, but also enables the kitten to sharpen the skills it will use for hunting, such as scooping, batting and pouncing.

The environmental impact of pet cats

The detrimental effect that pet cats can have on local wildlife is similar to that of feral cats or of the receding wild-cat species in the world. The results of one study suggest that as many as 75 to 100 million small mammals and birds are killed annually by pet cats in the UK alone! In this, perhaps the pet cat is simply filling the predator's niche – a niche left for a small, solitary carnivore due to the withdrawal or decline through loss of habitat of the native Scottish wild cat and other small hunters of rodents such as stoats and weasels, which cannot exist easily alongside humans.

In contrast, we have also prized the efforts of pet or factory cats at controlling rodents, and many highly successful cases are noted in the record books. Towser, a female cat born in a whisky distillery in Scotland, caught an average of three mice per day in her 23-year life-time – a working total of over 25,000! However, even this feat is perhaps outweighed by the great ratting cats. In the six years between 1927 and 1933, another female called Minnie more than earned her keep by catching 12,500 rats at the White City Stadium in west London. So you may yet come to appreciate your kitten's developing predatory skills, if you would prefer not to have mice and rats lurking in your home!

However, if you find the spectacle of dead birds upsetting, you may be able to reduce the carnage a little by not allowing your kitten out at dawn, dusk or night during the birds' nesting season. In some parts of Australia, all pet cats must be taken indoors by their owners at dusk and kept there until dawn, to reduce the threat that they pose to wildlife such as possums and the rare lyrebird. Owners face large fines if they fail to adhere to the law.

In the UK at least, although the predation is distressing to birds, bird lovers and cat owners, there is no evidence to suggest that the occasional high mortality of birds due to pet cats has had any damaging effect on even one species of bird. You simply have to learn to live with the fact that your cuddly kitten will one day be a fully grown and lethal predator.

The cat is a highly athletic creature, confident at leaping and climbing – sometimes to considerable heights. This agility enables it to view its environment from many different perspectives.

YOUR KITTEN'S EYE VIEW

Have you ever got down to the eye level of a toddler and wondered at how different the world looks – at how feet look so huge and adult heads so far away? Take this a little further down to ankle level and look afresh at your home and garden, as this is the angle from which your kitten (unless, of course, it is halfway up the curtains) will see.

However, although a kitten lives in the same physical environment as we do, it may perceive things in a very different way because of its heightened senses of hearing, smell and touch, and may be influenced by factors of which we are only vaguely aware. Remember that your small bundle of fur is, in fact, a developing predator, and that all its senses are highly tuned to ensure frequent success on hunting missions. Below is a brief outline of how the cat sees, hears, smells and feels the world around it – to the best of our limited understanding.

Confidence of movement

Although your kitten may dash about and bump into objects during a skittish five minutes, or may drop to the floor during a frantic rush to the top of the curtains, its athletic abilities give it a poise and balance way beyond the abilities of our own bodies – even the most clumsy cat can make our top human gymnasts look slow and cumbersome.

To an inquisitive young kitten, everything it sees is fascinating and worthy of investigation. Its highly developed senses allow it to perceive the world and be influenced by it in a very different way from a human.

A fully grown cat can leap to five times its height from a standing start with very little effort, climb a tree, walk without a wobble along the slimmest of fences, and bend and stretch to the envy of any yoga expert. A young kitten will not yet have mastered every trick to perfection, but all that dashing around, jumping in the air and climbing are practice for the time when the grace and speed of its actions will make it one of the most successful hunters in the animal kingdom.

Through feline eyes

The feline eye, although basically similar to that of other mammalian species, does have unique specialities of its own. It is thought that cats can see some colour, although their vision is mainly adapted to see

Meeting other species is all part of the learning process, and needs to begin during the all-important socialization phase (see pages 41–4) if a kitten is to grow up confident in any situation that it encounters.

well in very poor light and to be very sensitive to movement (because cats hunt mainly at twilight, when most of their rodent prey is on the move, they do not actually need to see in colour). Special nerve cells that are located in the cat's brain respond to the smallest movement, and the cat is then able to pinpoint this movement very accurately.

Behind the splendid colour of your kitten's eye (the iris) lies the pupil, with its light-sensitive layer of cells (the retina). A special layer of cells situated behind the retina (the tapetum) reflects back any light that has not been absorbed on its way through, so that the eye is given a second chance to intercept the image. It is this layer of cells – acting in the same way as a mirror – that is reponsible for the remarkable gold or green shine that we can see in a cat's eyes when they happen to be caught for a moment in a passing car's headlights.

These special adaptations of the eye, along with the ability to open the pupil very wide, allow your kitten to see perfectly well in what we would term 'darkness' – cats cannot in fact see in total darkness, but they can see in light approximately six times dimmer than we ourselves need to find our way about, and in light that sophisticated scientific instruments are barely able to detect.

The twitch of an ear

Your kitten has very mobile ears – they can swivel through 180 degrees, lie completely flat against the head or be extremely 'pricked', and they can even move in opposite directions at once. Although we tend to think of dogs as our keen-eared friends, the cat is sensitive to sounds of even higher frequency than the dog (a dog hears up to about 35 kHz, a cat to about 65 kHz).

Our ears are sensitive up to about 20kHz and so we miss many of the high-pitched squeaks and sounds made by small rodents, to which the cat is very attuned. Locating prey very accurately by sound means that a cat can move in swiftly, directly and silently, and not have to rely solely on sight to pinpoint its prey's position until it is close up. There are therefore probably all sorts of high-pitched sounds in your home of which you will be blissfully unaware, but which your kitten will be registering all the time.

The importance of touch

Watch your kitten investigating a new object, learning to play with prey or sneaking up on something strange. It will first touch the object rather timidly with its paw, then touch it again with a little more determination, and finally move in closer to investigate with its nose. The pads of the paw and the nose – both covered in soft skin and usually still pink in many kittens – are very sensitive to stimulation.

The pads are also very sensitive to vibration – indeed, deaf cats are thought to 'hear' with their feet, feeling vibrations and interpreting them in order to perceive what is going on around them. Strangely enough, although sensitive to touch the pads are not very responsive to the sensations of hot or cold, and this is probably the reason why some cats jump up on the hob of a cooker, seemingly oblivious to the heat that is radiating from it.

The nose and upper lip are the only parts of the cat's body that are very sensitive to temperature. Even a tiny newborn kitten will use its temperature-sensitive nose to 'home in' on the warmth of its mother, and will follow the temperature gradient to the warmest spot. A cat also uses its nose and lips to estimate the temperature of food, preferring to eat it at body temperature (as freshly killed prey would be) rather than chilled from a refrigerator.

If you look at your kitten with the light behind it you will notice whiskers on its upper lip, above the eyes and on the chin and elbows. These coarse hairs, called vibrissae, form a type of 'force field' of sensitivity which may be switched on by the tiniest touch or even by a slight breeze. The vibrissae sprout from a deeper layer of the skin than other hairs and

The learning experience is a mutual one. Given time, even the most unlikely of animals can become friends.

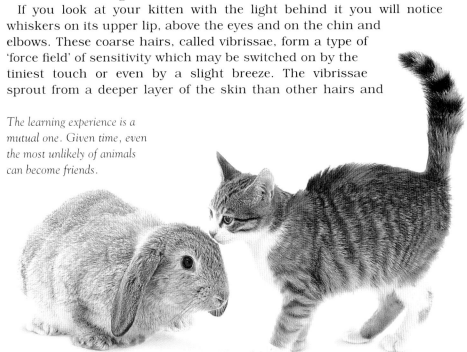

act as levers, magnifying any slight movement when they bend. By stimulating nerve endings they can provide detailed information on the kitten's surroundings, enabling it to 'feel' the presence of objects simply because of air currents circulating around them. The nerve impulses travel along the same path to the brain as information coming from the eyes, and the brain uses the two systems to build up a three-dimensional picture of the environment.

Whiskers are not static on the face, but are actually very mobile. For instance, if your kitten is frightened it may hold the whiskers close to its face to make itself seem smaller; when hunting, it may splay the whiskers far forward, using them as a 'third paw' to feel the prey in its mouth and ensure that it has the correct positioning for the killing bite to the nape of the neck.

The senses of smell and taste

A kitten may entertain itself for long periods with simple toys – over 10 types of object-play behaviour have been identified.

If you are beginning to get a feel for the world of your kitten, with its view of fairly drab colours but amazing night vision, its sensitive 'hearing' feet and 'seeing' whiskers, you are ready to enter the strange realm of scents. A cat can detect smells to the same intensity that we can see – in detail and in the smell equivalent of glorious technicolour – and relies on this sense as much as we do on our sight. Our own dull sense of smell makes it very hard to imagine a world of smells so intense that it must be like swimming through different colours, textures and tastes of fluids, receiving important information from them about the surroundings and even about who or what has passed that way.

Having investigated a new toy, a kitten may grasp, poke, bat or toss it into the air.

Unlike the dog – which hunts by scent – your kitten will use its eyes and ears for hunting, and its sense of smell more for the purposes of communication. The sense of smell functions to help the kitten to meet or to avoid other cats and, inadvertently, humans and other members of the household such as dogs. Just how its sense of smell helps it to communicate is outlined on pages 121–3.

Your kitten's tongue – which is also an essential implement for self-grooming – is very sensitive to temperature and taste. In fact, the cat is said even to be able to taste plain water, but perhaps not to experience the taste sensation of 'sweet'. This could be the reason why many cats do not like to drink water straight from the tap – with its added chlorine, fluorine and other chemicals – but will happily drink from a muddy puddle. Similarly, most cats are unexcited by the prospect of sweet items such as chocolate, which is understandable as there are very few sweet-tasting rodents about.

Objects that can be pulled along on a length of string are great favourites, and help to sharpen the kitten's reactions.

You may already be feeling a little overwhelmed by the feline senses, but another one to consider – which we cannot fully understand because it is lacking from our own physiology – is the vomeronasal organ (see page 44). This seems to enable a cat to concentrate smells and taste them at the same time, and therefore to extract much more information than would be possible by smell alone.

FELINE COMMUNICATION

Cats communicate via scent and body language, and sometimes vocally. With a little observation you can learn to gain an insight into what your kitten is feeling and what message it is trying to convey.

Talking smells

When you stroke your kitten, you are not only giving it a physical message but adding your smell to a complex mixture of scents that will give the kitten a sense of social grouping and home. A cat has areas of skin on its

Kittens are most actively involved in so-called 'social play' between the ages of nine and 14 weeks. The games may look at times more like fights, but will usually end amicably.

121

chin, lips, temples and at the base of its tail where some special subcutaneous glands produce an oily secretion specific to that individual (like a human fingerprint). It will use this scent to mark areas around it, as well as other cats, animals and people in its group. By stroking your kitten, you are spreading its scent and mixing it with your own, thus helping to create a communal smell comprising members of the household and the environment in which the kitten lives. In other words, your home will have a certain smell profile.

This is the reason why many cats become very upset when something new comes into the home. For instance, the smell of a new carpet is fairly strong even to us, so imagine what it does to the smell profile of your home, and how the highly sensitive nose of

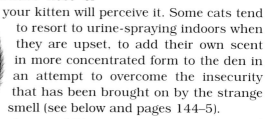

Even young kittens make use of the entire adult behavioural repertoire during their play activity: here, one kitten is rolling over in order to invite the other kitten to play.

your kitten will perceive it. Some cats tend to resort to urine-spraying indoors when they are upset, to add their own scent in more concentrated form to the den in an attempt to overcome the insecurity that has been brought on by the strange smell (see below and pages 144–5).

As your kitten grows up you may see it experimenting with marking by rubbing its face and lips against twigs in the garden, or on corners of items in the house. The purpose of this is to deposit scent from glands on its face. When the kitten rubs around your legs and head-butts you with delight when you are stroking it, it is also brushing you with scent. Another method of

All the movements that will be used for hunting are used in play: the kitten on the left has crouched down and pounced forward, surprising the other kitten into a retreat.

leaving a scent is by scratching. Glands situated between the pads of an adult cat's feet secrete a fluid which adds information to the visual mark left behind by scratching. Kittens often become very excited when they scratch, and will follow this with a mad dash around.

122

While rubbing and scratching are more subtle and intimate forms of communication between cats, the spraying of urine is more potent – the pungent smell of a tom cat's spray in particular is not easily ignored. Your kitten will not start to mark by spraying until it is sexually mature (usually at about six months of age – see page 150). Both male and female cats spray, but the desire to use this form of communication is greatly reduced by neutering.

Cats employ all these means to inform other cats of their movements; this allows them to 'time-share' their hunting territory and to meet up to reproduce if and when the time comes for mating.

Body language

Kittens are very good teachers when it comes to body language. In their play and hunting practice they often exaggerate the movements and the body language that are visible in a more subtle form in adult cats, and some of the most appealing of all aspects of a cat's behavioural repertoire are displayed during play. Kittens will put on a lively pantomime of hunting, courtship and fighting which may not be shown by older cats living in a peaceful household.

The roles are reversed every few seconds during the game, as first one and then the other kitten gains the advantage. Such games often only come to an end through exhaustion!

Boxing and ducking, the kittens' turned-back ears show that neither is quite sure what is going to happen next, but after a brief pause the rough and tumble will start again.

The aim of a cat's body language is to let another cat know its intentions in a given situation and, in most cases, to try to avoid conflict or injury. Unlike dogs, which live in groups in the wild

and have to learn to co-operate and signal their appeasement in certain circumstances, the cat is a solitary creature which can choose to be social or not if it wishes. It does not have the behavioural repertoire or facial language of the dog, and will usually flee or freeze in the face of danger. Only rarely, when it has no option, will it actually fight.

The cat uses its whole body to signal its feelings, although the main areas of communication are its eyes and ears, as well as its body position and size. These are all examined individually below, but the combination must be taken into account if we are to try to read the whole story.

Eye contact

This is essential for human beings, and it also plays a very important role in feline communication. However, prolonged eye contact or staring is an assertive act for a cat, and is often used by rival toms – for example, in an attempt to intimidate each other.

This kitten is frightened: it has erected the fur along its back and tail, and stands sideways to look bigger to its opponent.

Your kitten's eyes will also be good indicators of its mood. A narrowing or a widening of the eye can display interest, anger or fear, and the size of the pupil is not only governed by the amount of available light but also reacts to the kitten's emotions. A dilated pupil may be a sign of fear or arousal (you will also need to look at the

This kitten is feeling very defensive: note its flattened ears, raised fur, hissing reaction and body posture.

ears and the body to decide which). When your kitten is relaxed, it will probably not have its eyes wide open, but the eyelids may appear heavy and it may blink slowly as a sign of contentment. Blinking is also a reassuring signal between cats. If your kitten is frightened its pupils may be extremely dilated, with the eyes appearing almost black, giving a 'boggle-eyed' effect.

Ear movements

Your kitten's ears are one of its most important instruments of communication. Flattened ears, for instance, are normally a sign of fear – the kitten will usually also be trying to make its body smaller so that it is not seen as a threat, or simply to make itself less noticeable.

You will often notice your kitten's ears twitch if it is a little unsure of something, as though it is thinking about what to do. Licking the lips may also be a sign of anxiety, although a cat which sits with the tip of its tongue sticking out is usually relaxed and contented.

Use of the tail As well as being an important tool for balance, your kitten's tail is an excellent flag for communication, and its position and movement can tell you a great deal. Unlike a dog with a wagging tail, we all know that a cat with a swishing tail is not happy – in fact, quite the opposite. A swishing tail means that a cat is agitated and in emotional conflict, and is best left alone. When your kitten is happy to see you, it will greet you with its tail up – this is really so that you can investigate the scent produced under its tail, although fortunately we are oblivious to this.

If a cat feels seriously theatened by an attacker, it may become so defensive that the hairs on its tail become erect, making it bristle like a bottle brush. This is not often seen in an adult cat, but, when your kitten meets next door's dog for the first time, it may exhibit this use of the tail beautifully.

Cats in conflict with one another may hold their tails at a strange angle (rather like an inverted 'L'). This can be seen in kittens when they are at play, as can an inverted 'U' tail position – usually when they are indulging in a fast and furious game.

Body postures The whole body position will give you an indication of your kitten's mood. By erecting the hair along its back and tail, the kitten can make itself look significantly bigger than it actually is, which is useful both when on the attack and when trying to frighten off an animal which is trying to attack. The kitten may also stand sideways – again, to appear bigger – and then move sideways, keeping the whole body facing its opponent until it is safely out of harm's way. This crab-like motion is often seen during kitten play.

This kitten has been frightened by something and has raised the hair along its arched back. If the 'threat' does not disappear, the kitten will edge away using a crab-like movement.

In contrast, if your kitten is frightened by something, it may try to shrink down and look as small and unthreatening as possible, so as not to provoke an attack or draw attention to itself. Alternatively, it may arch its back in an attempt to make itself look bigger, and begin to edge away slowly with a sideways movement.

Cat talk

Your kitten will soon learn to miaow for attention, and will do it all the more if you leap into action – cats train us very well! They have a range of 'miaow' sounds, ranging from the pitiful and despondent (when they want something) to the extremely cross (if they do not get it). Experts are still studying feline sounds to try to establish how many there are and what each of them signifies, but, in the meantime, it is up to you to assess your own kitten's repertoire.

A kitten will hiss, spit and growl when it is frightened of something, but the sound that we enjoy best is the purr. All cats purr at the same frequency – 25 cycles per second – but exactly how they produce the sound still puzzles scientists, although many believe

During conflict a kitten may hold its tail at a strange angle, as here – this is known as the 'inverted L' tail position.

that it arises in the cardiovascular system rather than in the lungs or throat. Kittens purr when they are very tiny, and, as purring does not interfere with nursing, it can continue as a message between mother and kitten that all is well. The queen may also purr as she enters the nest to reassure her kittens.

Kittens purr when they play together, and when they are trying to encourage other kittens or even people to join in – perhaps to ingratiate themselves or to convey the idea of enjoyment. However and whenever they do it, we humans certainly have a soft spot for the contented purr, and hearing and feeling it must be one of the most rewarding of all the aspects of owning a kitten or cat.

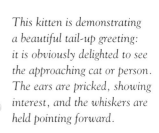

This kitten is demonstrating a beautiful tail-up greeting: it is obviously delighted to see the approaching cat or person. The ears are pricked, showing interest, and the whiskers are held pointing forward.

CHAPTER TWELVE

LEARNING AND TRAINING

A kitten will start learning things about its environment from the moment it is born. Initially it may only discover what feels warm and where to feed, but this basic awareness soon progresses to learning more about its mother and littermates, and about the world around it – including people.

As kittens grow older, they must learn about the world for themselves. The kittens in this litter are starting to become a real handful, and weaning needs to begin in earnest.

Life is a complex, sometimes difficult series of events and challenges. The animals which learn to cope with these challenges, and to face them in a non-confrontational yet adaptable way, are usually life's winners. Such individuals survive and thrive in their environment, and this, surely, is what makes the cat such a unique and successful creature. It has populated nearly every part of the world, made itself comfortable, found food to eat and, very often, found its way into our hearts and homes as well.

However, the adaptability of the cat has to be learned, and each and every young kitten needs to discover how to become flexible in an ever-changing environment, how to cope with life's demands and, most important of all, how to compromise.

LEARNING THE FIRST LESSON – WEANING

Studies of weaning in mammals have traditionally concentrated on the physical changes and nutritional demands of moving from milk to solid foods, but research recently carried out suggests that there may be more significance to weaning than simply what is on the menu.

A kitten learns all its social skills from its mother and siblings. For the first few weeks of life, it depends entirely on its mother for survival, and she provides food and warmth on demand. However, because the cat is a largely solitary species, a kitten must learn as quickly as it can to be independent of its mother and its litter-mates, so that it can also learn to hunt, kill and feed itself.

This transition – from total dependence to independence – needs to take place before the age of 18 to 20 weeks, when kittens in a wild environment would usually leave their mother and start to fend for themselves. This means that, during this period, the mother must teach her offspring to accept solid food and to become less dependent on her by gradually withdrawing her milk supply. From a behavioural perspective, weaning occurs in four stages.

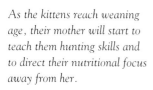

As the kittens reach weaning age, their mother will start to teach them hunting skills and to direct their nutritional focus away from her.

Stage one
This consists of 'continuous reinforcement': that is, the mother allows the kittens to feed – or to be rewarded – each and every time they approach her and root for milk.

Stage two
At three to four weeks old the kittens are much more capable and active, and will approach their mother and demand food in no uncertain terms. She now needs to leave the nest more frequently to feed herself, in order to be able to produce the increased quantity of milk that the rapidly growing kittens require.

However, on her return, despite the kittens' active demands, the queen may not always allow them to feed. Even if they do so she may get up and walk away after a brief period, letting the kittens simply fall off her teats. Really persistent kittens may even have to be nosed away, or may be dragged out of the nest as they cling to the teats for all they are worth. For the first time the kittens learn to experience rejection by their mother. This creates frustration, as they can clearly see the object of their desire, yet may not be permitted to have it.

Stage three

As we know, frustration increases vigour – in other words, we try harder to get what we want. Having failed in their attempts to get to their mother's milk, yet motivated by their frustration, the kittens start to experiment with different ways of getting food. It is at this stage that the mother starts to initiate an interest in prey by bringing stunned rodents back to the nest for the kittens to investigate.

Stage four

This allows the kittens to re-learn that their mother's approach no longer means milk, but signals food of a different kind. Not only has the process of weaning been completed, but the kittens have experienced the effect of frustration and learned to adapt their behaviour to obtain rewards as a result.

Coping with frustration through weaning is one of the first of many challenges that a kitten will face in its life. It is not always possible for any living being to have exactly what it wants, whenever it wants it, and learning this early on encourages cats to be adaptable and able to compromise – and, ultimately, to fit into family life more easily.

The kittens learn about their environment by making forays further and further away from their mother, but will soon dash back to her if alarmed.

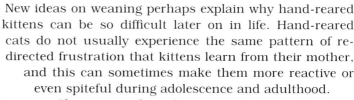

New ideas on weaning perhaps explain why hand-reared kittens can be so difficult later on in life. Hand-reared cats do not usually experience the same pattern of re-directed frustration that kittens learn from their mother, and this can sometimes make them more reactive or even spiteful during adolescence and adulthood.

If you ever face the prospect of hand-rearing kittens, seek help on how to instigate a weaning process that will expose them to behavioural experiences such as frustration. A member of the Association of Pet Behaviour Counsellors (in the UK), or of a similar organization in your country, may be able to advise you on this specialist subject.

LEARNING FROM LIFE

Like the vast majority of living creatures, cats will behave in certain ways because it benefits them to do so. A good rule of thumb to bear in mind when you are starting to train your kitten is: 'If it gets rewarded, it gets repeated.' However, rewards come in many shapes and forms, and what is a 'good thing' to one kitten may not be so to another, which is worth bearing in mind at all times during your kitten's upbringing. This is very important, because owners often unwittingly reinforce unwanted or undesirable behaviours in their cats, simply by rewarding them inadvertently. For instance, most cats will regard pleasurable physical contact as rewarding, but many will also view vocal contact from their owners, or even eye contact – being looked at – as worth working for.

Providing food is one of the best ways for a kitten's 'new mother' to form bonds with it. The kitten is now weaned and independent from the queen, and has learned to adapt its behaviour accordingly.

On the other hand, behaviours which go unrewarded will gradually extinguish, diminishing in frequency and intensity over a period of time; this is because there is little point in the cat investing energy in any action if it brings no benefit. However, do not forget the effects of frustration, and do use them to your advantage when training by delaying the provision of anticipated rewards. If you are trying to prevent your kitten doing something, and you take away the expected reward (such as food or your attention), remember that the behaviour may increase before it decreases as the kitten tries harder to get the reward.

TRAINING YOUR KITTEN

Cats are not small dogs – an obvious point, but one that is particularly relevant when talking about training. Dogs allow some humans to get away with thoughtless, compulsive and even punitive techniques to train them to do what they want. This is not necessarily because they want to 'please' us, as has been traditionally thought, but more probably because they simply cannot escape.

Most cats, on the other hand, are unlikely to put up with any training technique which does not fit their view of life by simply walking or running away. Cats do not have to put up with humans attempting to force them to perform specific actions, and do not have to put a brave face on the indignities of being trained by a clumsy owner. If they don't like it, they leave!

This characteristic will make training your kitten both challenging and enormously rewarding. If you can train a cat, you can train almost anything (even members of your family!) because you will have learned how to work with the animal, how to motivate it, and how to hone your timing skills so that your rewards are meaningful and effective.

Why train your kitten?

Teaching your kitten to do specific things when asked is valuable for many reasons. Some owners are reluctant to train their cats in any way, believing that it is demeaning to make them perform 'tricks'. When dealing with such an independent and dignified animal this is under-standable, but sensitive, fun training should never be demeaning.

Training your kitten to respond to you has a practical purpose. For instance, teaching it to come when called can be a life-saver, and will be vital if you ever need to locate it in a dangerous situation. In order for your kitten to become an accepted and much-loved member of the household, you also need to instil some guidelines about what is appropriate behaviour and what is not.

However, more than any other reason, training is important because it will strengthen the bond and enhance the relationship between you and your kitten. Training time for most cats means interaction. It is quality time that you are spending to stimulate your kitten's mental abilities, and to build on your relationship. Training that is fun also increases the confidence of many animals.

Success breeds success, and, the more enjoyable activities that your kitten takes part in with you, the more reinforcing – or rewarding – they will become. Good relationships, and good training, are built on mutual respect and communication. For many owners, training their new kittens to perform a range of simple actions by kind, gentle and effective methods is a true meeting of minds – you really do need to be open to the feline view of the world in order to be able to communicate effectively (see also pages 117–26).

Motivating your kitten to learn

As has already been mentioned, cats rarely do something for nothing. If you are aiming to teach your kitten a new exercise – even something as simple as coming when called, or using the cat flap – the kitten will have to work at learning something new, and the motivation for this effort needs to be apparent.

This 'salary' that you offer in return for your kitten's 'work' also needs to be attractive – it is no good offering a piece of dry cat food and expecting your kitten to turn back flips, unless it really loves dry cat food. In most instances, the rewards on offer for a new behaviour need to be special – the equivalent of the salary plus company car, in human terms!

Many cats will work hard for a small piece of fish, chicken or even a tiny piece of cheese. Many different cat treats are available from pet shops and supermarkets, and your kitten may love one of these. Novelty value also counts for a great deal. Offering your kitten a small piece of what it usually gets to eat for dinner is not likely to have the desired effect – after all, the kitten can simply wait until dinner time and have ten times as much for nothing.

If your kitten is not particularly motivated by food and is not tempted even by a special treat, a game with you, or a particular toy may have the desired effect. The general rule is to find something that your kitten really likes to provide motivation in the initial stages of training. It is also vital that you give the reward the moment your kitten performs the desired behaviour, as a delay of even a second will weaken its effect.

Taking things slowly

Any training, of any description, must be done at your kitten's pace. It is almost impossible to try to rush training a cat, and impatience could result in your kitten being put off the experience altogether.

Always break down the task into as many small stages as possible, and work towards each goal in a quiet and methodical way. Teaching your new kitten should be done without any distractions, and in a relatively quiet place. Other cats or dogs will almost always attempt to muscle in on the fun if they are aware that the kitten is receiving some extra attention from you, particularly if you are using food as a lure. It is therefore best to practise training on a one-to-one basis, which will also give your relationship with your kitten an opportunity to mature away from other pets.

Like us, cats can have off days. Your kitten may have been keen to play with you or to come to you quickly when you practised the day before, but may seem sluggish or bored the next time you try. Equally, you may not always be in the best of moods to begin a training session. If you have been stuck in traffic on the way home, or your kitten seems restless or disinterested, stop, have a break, and resume at another time. This so-called latent learning – the experience of having a break from learning a new behaviour, and then returning to it with a greater understanding the next time – often helps in training, usually when least expected. This makes taking rests between very short, very sweet training sessions vitally important.

What about punishment?

NEVER use physical punishment of any kind when interacting with your kitten. Punishment is counter-productive, will break down your relationship and will lead to resentment, fear and stress on both sides.

An owner sometimes claims that a cat 'knows it has done wrong' after behaving inappropriately. Sadly, this is a misinterpretation of the cat's body language, as no animal is able to understand the complexity of our human values. A cat cannot be expected to comprehend the difference between scratching the curtains or the sofa if its scratching post is made of similar material, nor that the best pot plant in the corner was not put there for indoor toileting.

A cat which behaves in inappropriate ways often learns to associate its owner's presence – particularly a stern face or tone of voice, or an aggressive approach – as threatening. It may cower or run away, but this does not indicate 'guilt' as we might experience it, as the link between the cat's own behaviour and the person's anger is rarely made. Instead, the cat is simply showing fear at the owner's attitude.

If your kitten does scratch the sofa, an angy reaction on your part – shouting or smacking, for instance – might stop the problem on that occasion, but the kitten is likely to do it again when you are not there. Instead, you need to interrupt the unwanted behaviour in some way. A sharp hissing sound will quickly distract most cats, as will a sudden noise such as clapping your hands. Try to avoid your kitten associating the interruption with you, so that it imagines the interruption to be a direct result of its actions.

Coming when called

One of the most vital lessons that you need to teach your kitten is to come when you call its name. This can save endless hours of worry and energy in the long term: a kitten which responds quickly and willingly when you call will be far easier to locate than one which ignores you, and you will always be able to discover its whereabouts (provided of course that it is within earshot). You should teach this lesson at an early stage, as it will be very useful if and when you let your kitten outdoors for the first time (see pages 77–8).

In an emergency, a cat which comes when called can also be removed from danger, or 'rescued'. Cats are notorious for wandering into sheds, garages or other inviting places, only to become trapped when someone unwittingly closes the door on them. In this situation, you will at least have some chance of locating your kitten if it knows its name when you call, and responds by calling back or by trying to get to you.

Last but not least, it is also enormously satisfying to call your kitten's name out of the back door, to hear a faint call in response from somewhere in the distance, and then to see the kitten bounding over the garden wall in anticipation of reaching you.

1 The way to most cats' hearts is through their stomachs! This means that the easiest way to start teaching your kitten to come when called – in other words, to provide the motivation for the kitten to do so – is to make a strong association with its name and food.

When your kitten is close by, call its name, then immediately offer something delicious such as a sumptuous titbit, or a tasty meal. Call the kitten's name every time you are going to do this, and keep your tone of voice light and pleasant. Words or sounds of two syllables seem to have more of an activating impact on many animals, while single, flat-sounding tones appear to have a slowing or calming effect. If your kitten's name has two syllables in any case, simply use that; if not, it may be helpful to add another sound to it. For example, 'Tig-ger' is easy to call out of the back door, while 'Blue' naturally becomes 'Blue-y'!

Initially, you should only call your kitten when it is actually in view, just to build up the association. Watch for your kitten turning its head towards you in anticipation of something pleasant happening, and then coming over to you. Remember to give the reward the moment you get this response.

2 Start to move further away before calling, until your kitten will come running even when you are out of sight. Intersperse rewarding with food, games or affection at this stage. Many kittens will come simply for company or affection, and this makes training them easy at an early age; others are more independent and need to be offered a bigger inducement. Whatever your kitten's personality, always make coming to you a pleasurable experience.

3 If you wish to sharpen your kitten's recall even further, start to reward only the fastest or best responses. You can even put your kitten on to a random reward schedule as a final stage of training.

One word of warning. NEVER call your kitten to you and then 'punish' it in any way. As has already been discussed (see pages 117–21), cats perceive the world in different ways from us, making some experiences appear to be punishing from a feline point of view, even if not from ours. Errors to avoid are calling your kitten in order to put it in a carrier before going to the vet, or to carry out a procedure which the kitten dislikes, such as giving medicine.

One poor owner who had worked extremely hard for about five weeks to establish and maintain her kitten's recall on command was forced to start all over again after calling the kitten to her, putting it on a table and spraying it with flea spray! Cats have long memories, and the association to your kitten of its name and an unpleasant experience can remain firmly fixed for a long time to come.

Much like dogs, the way to most cats' hearts is through their stomachs. Use a treat or a morsel of favourite food to encourage your kitten to come when you call, and to increase its interactions with you and the other members of your family.

By your propping open the cat flap with a pencil or securing it with a piece of tape, the kitten will gain in confidence and see that it may enter and leave as it wishes. Encourage your kitten with morsels of food and plenty of praise initially, as the first step can be a little daunting.

Using the cat flap

Once your kitten has completed its primary vaccinations (see page 87) you may decide to allow it in and out of the house as it pleases, and many people find that a cat flap answers this need admirably. However, to many kittens the sight of a strange, swinging door – heralding a route to a daunting new world outside – is a terrifying experience. Always build your kitten's confidence about going outdoors (see pages 77–8) before training it to use the flap. After all, it will not be very rewarding for your kitten to learn to use the flap, only to discover that the result of pushing it open is becoming lost or being attacked by another cat waiting on the doorstep.

Some confident kittens learn the knack of pushing a cat flap open very quickly, as their desire to come in or go out motivates them to do so. Other, more anxious individuals take a long time to discover that the movement, noise and sight of the flap are not dangerous and that they will not come to any harm by pushing it.

As with all training exercises, you should work on one stage at a time, and only continue at your kitten's pace. Never try to push the kitten through the flap, or to push its paws or head against the door in an attempt to show it what to do. You could put your kitten off for life by frightening it in this way.

1 Your kitten needs to understand that the flap is now an entrance and exit to the home. This can be a strange concept for some cats to cope with at first, particularly if they have not already seen other animals using the flap. Prop the flap open with a pencil or a piece of tape so that your kitten can look out through it. Allow as much time as it takes for the kitten to become comfortable with this idea – if you sit down nearby, you will give it extra confidence.

2 Most kittens find the first experience of going through a cat flap less frightening if they are entering their area of security rather than leaving it, so gently placing your kitten at the entrance to the open flap from the outside is usually best at first. Ask someone to help you by holding the kitten outside the door, while you encourage it to come through the hole by luring with a food treat and calling its name. Remember to give your kitten the food the instant it comes through the flap.

Once the kitten seems happy and confident about going through the cat flap when it is propped open, take away the pencil or tape and encourage it to push the flap open itself. Dangling a toy invitingly on the other side of the flap should help to tempt the kitten through if it is a little reluctant at first.

3 Once the kitten has mastered coming in, squat on the outside of the door and call the kitten through from inside the house. Praise and reward any attempts to walk through initially, then give the food treat and plenty of praise for a confident walk through the open flap.

4 Prop the flap so that it is only half-open. This will show the kitten that, although it is still an entrance/exit hole, a hint of an obstruction needs to be overcome to get the reward. Encourage your kitten to push gently against the flap to gain access to the food.

5 Once the kitten is confident about pushing the flap like this – from both sides of the door – lower the flap a little more and let it experiment again. In no time at all, the kitten will be popping in and out of the flap just for the fun of it!

'No-exit' signs If you plan to keep your kitten in at night – or at any other time (see Chapter Seven) – it is a good idea to signal the times when the cat flap cannot be used as an exit. If you think about it, although you may be able to see quite well that the flap is locked in place, your kitten will simply not understand why it cannot push the flap open when only minutes before a single shove with its front paws worked beautifully.

Placing a 'signal' next to or across the flap is a useful strategy, as your kitten will learn to associate the signal with an inability to open the flap, and so will give up excessive attempts to break out. The signal can be anything that is convenient – such as a towel hanging nearby or a piece of board placed across the flap – but must be consistent right from the start. As your kitten starts to get the idea, the 'no-exit' signal can gradually be reduced in size or moved further away.

Walking on a harness and lead

If you do not plan to allow your kitten free access to the outside world, training it to walk on a harness and lead can provide a reasonable compromise between freedom and safety (see also page 78). You may, for example, decide that you wish to exercise your kitten on a harness solely in the comparative safety of your garden, so that it can explore the outside world but is protected from other cats, dogs and traffic.

Some owners manage to train their cats to go for walks further afield without becoming at all fearful, but this takes a great deal of gradual, patient practice and training from an early age. In contrast to what some people may think, walking a cat on a harness is not the same as exercising a dog on a collar and lead. In fact, more often than not, it is the cat which decides where it wishes to walk and the owner who follows behind.

If you would like to accustom your kitten to wearing a harness for outdoor exercise, you must start early. Make the experience rewarding and soothing for the kitten, using food and plenty of praise.

Cats can easily become panic-stricken if they are frightened and find that they cannot run away. For this reason it is essential to accustom your kitten to wearing a harness, and to the feeling of the lead being attached, very gradually.

1 The process of training must be carried out extremely carefully, and you must always stop immediately if your kitten appears to become at all distressed by the restriction of the harness. The first step is to accustom your kitten to the sensation of wearing the harness without the lead attached. Put on the harness very gently and then leave it in place for a few seconds while you play together; or feed the kitten in the harness.

2 Gradually extend the periods that the harness is worn in the house, taking things entirely at your kitten's pace. It should remain completely relaxed throughout, and this may take some time to achieve. As when you first began the training, if the kitten at any point becomes distressed by the restriction of the harness, remove it and try again at another time.

3 Attach a fairly short, very lightweight length of cord or string to the harness (the use of cord or string instead of a lead at this stage is so that the kitten – and, even more importantly, you – can become accustomed to the feel of having something attached to the harness). Holding the end of the cord very gently, allow your kitten to wander at will for a few seconds – preferably lured by a food treat held in your other hand. If the kitten starts to move away from you, either drop the cord or follow the kitten calmly. Never attempt to jerk or pull on the cord as a means of restraint, or allow the kitten to begin playing with the end of the cord (or later the lead). In doing so, it could easily pull on the cord, tightening the harness around itself and panicking at such a sudden, self-inflicted restriction.

Once your kitten is completely accustomed to wearing the harness without the lead attached, you can progress to using a very lightweight length of cord or string, and then to using a proper lead. Practise around the house at first, and only venture out of doors once you are quite sure that your kitten is completely relaxed with the feel of this restriction on its natural movement.

4 When your kitten is happy to walk on the harness and cord, swap the cord for a light lead. Practise in short, fun sessions, walking around the house, and always reward your kitten for good and confident behaviour. Once the kitten is truly relaxed about the harness and lead, venture out into the garden to allow your kitten some of the benefits of outdoor stimulation, without the perils. Going out beyond the boundaries of the garden – unless perhaps to a very quiet park – is not advisable, as something unexpected could occur and frighten your kitten.

Training your kitten to retrieve

This exercise is very easy to teach some cats, but more challenging with others. Carrying prey is a natural behaviour, and many breeds are adept at chasing, picking up and carrying toys, and then bringing them back to their owners to be thrown again. This provides wonderful stimulation for an active cat – particularly one living indoors – as it exercises hunting skills which may not have many other outlets.

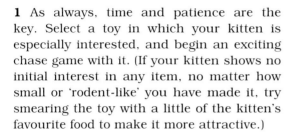

1 As always, time and patience are the key. Select a toy in which your kitten is especially interested, and begin an exciting chase game with it. (If your kitten shows no initial interest in any item, no matter how small or 'rodent-like' you have made it, try smearing the toy with a little of the kitten's favourite food to make it more attractive.)

Toys are loved by children and kittens alike, and they will play happily together for long periods. As a first step, the child should get the kitten interested in the toy, before throwing it – the kitten will follow the movement.

2 As soon as your kitten runs after the toy and picks it up, call the kitten to you. Offer a food lure, or an identical toy to the one that you have already thrown, as a 'swap' for the retrieved item. Do not ever be tempted to engage your kitten in a tug of war with any item in an effort to get it back. Your kitten is the one with the claws and may win the struggle, which will simply encourage it to run off more quickly with the article the next time, or not to return with it at all.

Once your kitten seizes the toy, call it to you, offering a piece of food or another toy. Many kittens love this game, and learn to retrieve very well.

CHAPTER THIRTEEN

PREVENTING BEHAVIOURAL PROBLEMS

Your kitten will make new discoveries every waking minute of every day. In the same way that it learns about its surroundings by trial and error, and by watching others, it will be constantly discovering what feels good and what does not, what actions will result in getting delicious things to eat, and what will make you reward it with your undivided attention.

Although cats usually scratch to sharpen their claws, or leave a scent mark using a branch or post, they will happily scratch indoors too – the carpet can be a great favourite if a designated scratching post is not provided.

Cats are themselves exceptional teachers, and many have their owners trained and reliable within only a few days of arriving in their new homes. Most of us are more than happy to be 'owned', loved and trained by our cats – it is part of what makes them such fascinating and independent personalities – but some tasks that our cats set us to do may be less enjoyable than others.

For instance, most cats have their owners trained to give them affection when they ask for it. The deliberate and distinctive approach – tail up, possibly a miaow along the way, and a quick rub – all ensure that any human with a heart is stroking, cooing and talking to the cat within seconds. Many cats also ask their owners for food, or games, by communicating in a way that the owner understands. If your kitten rubs against your legs, gives plaintive chirrups and looks pleadingly at the food dish at five o'clock in the afternoon, you may consider it cute and clever. However, if it leaps on to your head at three o'clock in the morning, miaows so loudly and persistently that you cannot possibly sleep, or deliberately knocks ornaments off the mantelpiece in order to be fed or petted, it is quite another matter.

PREVENTION IS BETTER THAN CURE

As a general rule, it will be much easier to train your kitten positively – in other words, to do certain things – rather than to teach it not to do something once it has learned an undesirable habit. As already discussed (see page 133), punishment is never a solution to any problem. Whether physical or vocal, it will almost always be associated with the last event that occurred – often your appearance – and rarely with the kitten's own behaviour. It is highly likely to lead to conflict in the kitten's mind about your presence, causing more stress and therefore an exacerbation of the original problem.

Unwanted behaviours in cats are nearly always natural behaviours that simply seem inappropriate to us. Many are also learned behaviours which have often been inadvertently taught by owners. The following are therefore two vital ways to prevent the occurrence of problems.

Start as you mean to go on

Try not to allow your kitten to do things that you may not appreciate later on. For example, if you habitually place its feeding bowl on a specific work surface, the kitten will build an association that the work surface is a good place to be. From its point of view, one work surface looks very much like the rest, so it is then hardly fair to blame the kitten if it decides to find out what the other work surfaces, cooker top and kitchen shelves have to offer. Of course, if the kitten finds these 'forbidden' surfaces unrewarding, it may decide to stick to the only one associated with food. On the other hand, a kitten which explores a different work surface for the first time and finds the Sunday roast there for the taking is extremely likely to repeat that behaviour.

Kittens will be kittens

Equally important in preventing problems is to anticipate your kitten's natural – and often essential – behaviours, and to provide a practical and appropriate outlet for them.

All cats need to be able to perform certain everyday functions in order to maintain their physical health. These include the following:
• Eating
• Drinking
• Toileting (including territory marking with urine and/or faeces)
• Scratching
• Self-grooming
• Resting

Some of these behaviours may seem almost too obvious to be examined, but thinking about them in some detail can be very enlightening.

Eating Of course your kitten needs to eat, but have you ever thought about what it might be like to eat too little, too much, the wrong type of food, or to eat in a frightening place? One behavioural horror story told of an owner who placed her kitten's food dish next to that of the family's eight-month-old Labrador retriever. She told the vet that she could not understand why her kitten would not eat and was so thin, despite the fact that she kept putting food down for it.

Prevent behavioural problems by feeding appropriate food, at set times during the day, in a place in which your kitten will feel secure and comfortable. Give the kitten its own food dish, and monitor its eating patterns. Stay in the vicinity and talk to your kitten, and let food help to build the bond between you.

Try not to give in to your kitten's demands for food at all times of the day and night, or they will quickly become a habit. If the kitten always seems to be hungry, ask your vet's advice – it could be that you are not feeding enough, or that the kitten is suffering from intestinal worms (see page 91).

Drinking Cats are very individual in their need and taste for water. Some love to drink running water straight from a tap or hosepipe, and will not drink water if it is standing in a bowl. Others appear to need very little water, and may fulfil all their requirements from licking dew from leaves in the garden, or from their food.

Some cats are very fussy about the freshness of their drink, as well as their food. If you allow water to stand in a bowl for more than about 24 hours, do not be surprised if your kitten decides that water in a glass, or even out of the toilet bowl, looks more appetizing. Keep a close eye on your kitten's daily water intake. A sudden increase could mean a health problem, so contact your vet if you are concerned.

Toileting However obvious it may seem, a kitten which has not yet been vaccinated, and therefore cannot go outside, will need a toilet somewhere indoors. Do not place a litter tray some-where so inappropriate, or inaccessible, that the kitten learns to go to the toilet elsewhere.

Always provide fresh, clean drinking water for your kitten, especially during periods when it has no access to outdoor and other sources of water.

Common sense is your best guide here. You would not like to eat your dinner in the toilet, and neither do cats, so placing your kitten's food a respectful distance from the litter tray is an essential requirement. Equally, your kitten needs to feel secure while on the tray, and must be protected while in this vulnerable position from the advances of children, dogs and other cats.

Another factor almost guaranteed to put your kitten off toileting on the tray is being grabbed while there in order to be given medicine. Even though this may be the only time in the day when your kitten keeps still long enough for you to hold on to it, resist the temptation and administer medicine or other treatment well away from the tray.

Your kitten could decide that the soil in a pot plant looks more inviting than using the litter tray, or, once it is allowed outdoors, venturing outside on a cold winter's morning. Again, avoiding the occurrence of the problem at the start will be better than trying to solve it after the event, so cover the soil in plant pots with gravel, or even with a sheet of plastic food wrap, as a temporary measure.

Scent-marking with urine from a squatting position. The cat squirts a small volume of urine on to a horizontal surface, thus leaving a message about itself for other passing cats.

Territory marking If a cat feels under threat in its territory and needs to feel more secure, it may begin to 'mark' in and around the home, using urine or faeces, once it approaches the onset of sexual maturity (see also page 150). Both male and female cats, whether neutered or not, may do this. The marks that are left may be urine patches deposited from a squatting position on flat surfaces, or sprayed urine (generally on vertical surfaces); or they may be faeces left in open places (middening).

As the marking is often carried out by cats in an effort to make themselves feel more secure, punishment will be especially counter-productive. It also means that cats frequently try to link their own smell with that of their 'protectors' – in other words, with their owners. It is therefore not uncommon for cats to mark with urine, faeces or both on areas that we find particularly disconcerting. Clothing (or other items which smell of us), furnishings and even the middle of the duvet are relatively common targets.

In all cases of indoor toileting, the scent of the cat's own urine is likely to lead it back to the same place to mark again, so removing all traces is essential. Cleaning the area with any product which smells good to you but simply masks the smell to your kitten, will make it think that another cat has marked over the top! Cleaning all areas with a solution of biological detergent is the most effective way to break down the proteinaceous compounds in urine, and you should follow this by light agitation with a brush and low-grade alcohol – such as a solution of surgical spirit – to remove any further fatty deposits (check for colour-fastness of furniture or fabric dyes by cleaning a hidden corner first).

There are many reasons why cats engage in inappropriate indoor soiling. Some of these include the fear of their core territory being invaded from external sources – either by another cat, such as the local tom, or by other animals. Some cases involve stress from a source from within the home – such as direct competition for sleeping areas, food or even the owner's attention – between two or more cats.

In almost every case, the cause of the anxiety or frustration needs to be explored and removed. This may be as simple as blocking up the cat flap so that next door's adult cat cannot chase your kitten indoors, but marking generally has a number of causative factors, and finding the root of these is essential. Success in treating problems nearly always lies in getting help early. Take the kitten to your vet to ensure that it is not suffering from any medical problem that could be causing the behaviour. If all is well physically, ask your vet for a referral to a qualified cat-behaviour specialist as soon as possible.

Scratching All cats have a biological need to scratch, and the action is a very deliberate and necessary one. Scratching helps to manicure the claws, is a fundamental method of scent communication between felines, and makes a cat feel more secure in that environment. In order to preserve your best furniture, and to ensure that your kitten has an outlet for this natural behaviour, you must provide it with a suitable scratching post (see pages 51–2).

Although some scratching is essential for all domestic felines, if a cat is anxious or stressed it will feel the need to scratch other objects as well as its designated post, and may do so in several locations around the home. If your kitten is insistent on using many different areas and items of furniture for scratching, there may be an anxiety problem. This should be investigated as soon as possible so that it can be resolved quickly, so ask your vet for advice; he or she may decide to refer you on to a cat-behaviour specialist.

Self-grooming It is estimated that a healthy adult cat may spend up to 30 per cent of its time engaged in grooming its own coat. This is mainly a kind of 'combing' with the tongue, rather than washing, but cats can also cool themselves by smearing their coats with saliva and allowing it to evaporate.

If your kitten is not grooming itself regularly, it may be suffering from an illness of some kind or from severe stress. Equally, over-grooming, in which a cat may groom itself so excessively that it pulls its own coat out, may well be a sign of illness or anxiety. Always have your kitten checked by your vet in such a case, and referred to a cat-behaviour specialist if necessary.

Resting Your kitten needs a designated place in the home – or several places – in which it can rest peacefully. One of the major causes of stress in cats, particularly those which live an entirely indoor existence, is being unable to remove themselves from the hubbub of daily life to find somewhere safe and quiet to sleep.

Cats love high places – they feel secure in being able to watch the world go by from above, and providing such a sanctuary for your kitten is essential if you have young children, dogs or other cats. Even where comfortable resting areas are available, some cats will perceive that there are not enough to go around and may refuse to share with another cat in the household. Disputes may occur over specially favoured spots, such as by the fire, but confrontations can often be avoided by providing enough prime sites to keep all members of the household happy.

Providing stimulation

In addition to the basic natural behaviours that have been described above, the following activities will all be fundamental to your kitten's behavioural repertoire:
• Acting out predatory sequences
• Exploring
• Exercising (including climbing, jumping and running)
• Social contact
These behavioural needs must all be catered for, in order to help prevent the development of behavioural problems.

Cats need to play, to act out predatory sequences and to explore. Each of these activities provides all-important mental stimulation, as well as physical exercise. If you do not provide your kitten with an appropriate outlet for its hunting skills, chasing behaviours and pouncing abilities, it will still practise them – but perhaps on you instead (see pages 114–15)! Many of the aggression cases presented to cat-behaviour specialists are directly linked to a lack of stimulation in the cats' environment. Of course, cats given the freedom to go outside as and when they wish will tend to find their own stimulation and gain exercise by performing natural activities – climbing trees, running and jumping – even if they are not particularly proficient hunters.

One recent study has suggested that the minimum area used on a day-to-day basis by a semi-feral urban cat is 200 sq m (240 sq yds). However, more important than the space available is the complexity of the cat's environment. Your kitten needs to be able to explore, and to find its home full of interesting objects and areas which can cater to its three-dimensional perception.

This means that you must provide the opportunity for your kitten to climb up and run along high surfaces, as well as producing novel and stimulating objects for investigation and play. Even an object as simple as a safe cardboard box is new and different. 'Puzzle feeders' of various descriptions are also available, and mean that the kitten has to 'work' in order to get its food.

Introducing a wide variety of toys will help to enrich your kitten's lifestyle if it is kept indoors, although many cats also like their owners to interact with them as they play. Cats need contact with people, or another cat, and 'quality time' spent with your kitten is vital. You may feel better for it, too!

Getting expert help

If you are experiencing any kind of behavioural problem with your kitten, ask your vet to refer you to a qualified cat-behaviour specialist. In the UK, the specialist should be a member of the Association of Pet Behaviour Counsellors (see page 158 for contact details). If you live outside the UK, there may be a similar regulatory body for behaviour specialists in your country.

If you need help with your kitten, try to arrange it as quickly as possible, as early treatment is always likely to be more successful than attempting to correct an already well-established problem.

CHAPTER FOURTEEN

GROWING UP

K ittens grow up fast. Within a few weeks of birth they are fully mobile and starting to take solid food; by eight weeks they should be completely weaned and ready to go to their new homes if they are non-pedigrees (pedigree kittens generally stay with their breeders for 12 weeks – see page 16). Unlike a puppy within a dog pack in the wild, which will be helped, looked after and fed by other members of the group until it can join in the hunt, a kitten must learn very quickly to look after itself and to catch its own prey. It will have to be a successful hunter by the age of 18–20 weeks, so it has little time for kittenhood.

MILESTONES OF DEVELOPMENT

Comparing the age of a kitten with the equivalent stage of a child's development will show you just how quickly your kitten is growing up. In its first eight weeks, a kitten develops from a tiny creature, unable to walk and with poor senses of hearing and sight, to a lively, agile animal which can eat solid food and is learning to hunt using precision hearing and eyesight. Within eight weeks the kitten has developed as much as a one- to two-year-old child; by four months old it will have mastered the basis of adult communication, equivalent to that of a four- to five-year-old child.

A kitten must develop rapidly – from complete dependence at birth to being able to move, feed and comprehend like an adult cat in just a few months. This two-week-old kitten is barely mobile, and will call to its mother for help if it falls out of the nest.

The next major stage in kitten development is sexual maturity, which occurs at approximately six months of age (see page 150) – and represents the equivalent development of a 12- or 13-year-old child. Indeed, a six-month-old kitten is said to be 75 per cent grown, so the comparison seems a fairly accurate one. This may also explain all those adolescent frolics and games that kittens play, and all the trouble they can get into at this particularly demanding age!

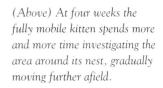

By the time a kitten is one year old, scientists consider it to be the equivalent of a 15-year-old person. At 14 months it is like an 18-year-old person – fully grown physically but with a good deal still to learn. By the time it reaches two years old it is thought to be rather grown up, and the equivalent of a 24-year-old person. From that stage onwards, if you add four years for every year that your cat lives, you will be able to calculate its approximate equivalent in our human years.

On average, cats live to about 14 years of age, which is the equivalent of 72 human years. However, thanks to the expert veterinary care that is now available – combined with good nutrition and dedicated owner care – many cats are now surviving for considerably longer than this, and even 20-year-old felines (equivalent to 96-year-old people) are not uncommon.

Cats are in fact unusual in that they live a long time for their size – longer than any other of our small domestic pets.

(Above) At four weeks the fully mobile kitten spends more and more time investigating the area around its nest, gradually moving further afield.

(Below) By nine weeks the kitten is already able to jump and move like an adult, and is starting to put basic hunting sequences together during play.

At six months old, the cat is the equivalent of an adolescent human. If you do not plan to breed from your kitten, you must have it neutered before it becomes sexually mature.

NEUTERING YOUR KITTEN

Your kitten will reach sexual maturity – in other words, be capable of producing kittens itself – from the age of about six to seven months, although exactly when this occurs can vary considerably.

The onset of sexual maturity in a non-pedigree kitten is thought to be weight-related, so that females first come into season when they weigh 2.3–2.5 kg (5–5½ lb) at about seven months of age, while males begin the change when they are 1 kg (2¼ lb) heavier and sometimes a month or two older.

In pedigree cats, the timing is more variable. For example, a Siamese queen may come into season at five months, whereas a Persian may not do so in the first year. The timing also depends on when a queen was born. A cat born in early spring may come into season that autumn, but one born later in the year may not do so until the next spring.

Well before your kitten is likely to reach sexual maturity, you must think about whether or not you would like it to parent a litter of kittens. If you do decide that you would like to breed from the kitten later, when it is old enough, consult your vet before going ahead – breeding is a great responsibility and not a decision to be made lightly. If you do not wish to breed from your kitten, you will need to have it neutered.

Spaying

Until recently it was suggested that all female cats should be allowed to have one litter before being spayed (the reasons for this were never clear, and were probably based on human needs rather than those of the cat – see page 28), but this is now considered totally unnecessary.

A female cat will only have the desire to mate when she comes into season (also called a 'heat'), at which time she will begin to 'call'. The use of the word call will become obvious once you have heard a female cat making it known to the world that she is looking for a tom.

Owners of the ordinarily vocal Siamese in particular will soon get the message – again and again!

A cat will keep coming into season every three weeks or so during the breeding season unless she becomes pregnant, so simply keeping your kitten indoors to avoid pregnancy will be a noisy business. One option is to ask your vet to administer a hormone treatment to prevent the kitten from coming into season, but doing this could cause fertility problems if you wish to breed from her later, and is in any case not recommended as a long-term solution.

If you do not wish to breed from your female kitten, the best option is spaying. Most people do not want the responsibility of a litter of kittens, not just because of the work involved but because of the difficulty in finding good homes for them – there are already far too many unwanted cats looking for loving homes. Once spayed, your kitten will not come into season, and will be spared any of the diseases associated with the uterus or ovaries which may occur in later life, as well as the risks associated with pregnancy and birth.

Spaying means surgically removing the uterus and ovaries under a general anaesthetic (your vet will ask you to withhold all food from your kitten after its dinner on the evening prior to the day of the anaesthetic). The fur at the operation site will be shaved, and an incision made through the skin, muscle and peritoneum (the lining membrane of the abdomen). The ovaries and uterus will then be removed and the incision closed. Your kitten should be able to return home the same day, and will need to return to have the skin stitches removed after about a week (unless soluble suture material is used, in which case the stitches will gradually dissolve on their own).

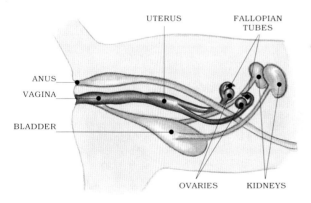
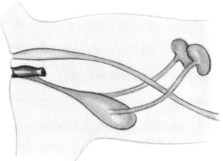
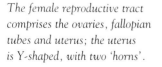

The female reproductive tract comprises the ovaries, fallopian tubes and uterus; the uterus is Y-shaped, with two 'horns'.

During spaying, the ovaries, fallopian tubes and uterus are removed through an incision made along the mid-line of the abdomen or in the flank.

Castration

As a male kitten matures, it will start to behave like a tom. An intact (uncastrated) tom cat has a very different lifestyle to that of his neutered counterpart – while he may be very affectionate to human companions, his priorities lie elsewhere, and he may spend a great deal of time patrolling his territory, which can stretch over a considerable area, fighting off rivals and looking for females.

The life of an intact tom is often rather rugged and likely to be considerably shorter than the life of a castrated male. Not only is the intact tom likely to become injured in fights with other cats in his territory, but he will be at much greater risk of infectious diseases such as feline leukaemia virus infection and feline immunodeficiency virus (see pages 89–91), which can be passed on via bites.

Although all cats – neutered or not – will usually spray around their territory (see pages 144–5), an intact tom may be more likely to do so indoors. The urine produced will also be extremely pungent and cannot be ignored – inside or out!

If you have never seen a cat spray, watch from your window when one passes through your garden. Notice how he sniffs posts and places where other cats may have been – you may see him lift his head and seem to draw back his lips as he smells and tastes the air, using the vomeronasal organ to identify which cat passed by and when (see page 44). When the cat comes across such a scent – for instance, on a wooden post – he may turn around with his tail next to the post, and you will see his hind feet paddle up and down a little and his tail quiver slightly. In that moment the cat has squirted a small volume of urine, mixed with a combination of hormones and odours, on to the post at cat-nose level, so that the next passing cat will know that he has been there. In other words, spraying is an extremely effective method of feline communication.

Urine-spraying may not be a problem in the garden, but it can be very offensive when it happens inside the house. Most people prefer to neuter their toms to help prevent this, as well as to ensure that the cats do not roam too far or become injured in fights. This is also the decision of responsible owners who do not wish their cats to sire unwanted litters of kittens.

Ideally, you should have your kitten castrated at an early age (between six and nine months), before urine-spraying and the other behavioural changes start to occur (castration removes testosterone, which is the primary motivating hormone for these behaviours). If you leave castration too late, your kitten may continue to exhibit some behaviours – such as spraying indoors – because they have become learned as well as instinctive.

Castration involves surgically removing part of the vas deferens and both testicles under a general anaesthetic. It does not usually require stitches, and the cat will have recovered well by the following day.

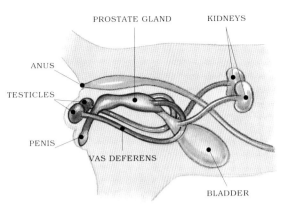

PROSTATE GLAND   KIDNEYS

ANUS

TESTICLES

PENIS

VAS DEFERENS

BLADDER

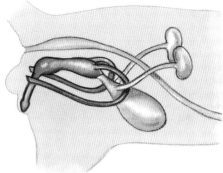

The male reproductive tract:
the two testicles lie in a skin
sac called the scrotum, and are
connected to the penis via the
vas deferens (spermatic cord).

Castration removes part of the vas
deferens and both testicles. This is
done though a tiny incision made
at the base of the scrotal sac, and
stitches are seldom necessary.

Post-operative care

When your kitten comes home after being spayed or castrated, keep it warm and comfortable in a soft, clean bed in a quiet area, with a litter tray available. Offer a drink of fresh water and, after a few hours, a small meal of white fish or chicken. Your vet will advise you whether you need to keep the kitten indoors overnight or longer.

Discourage your kitten from jumping or playing wildly for the first few days. Most male cats recover from castration extremely quickly, as it is not a major operation. Even though spaying is a major internal surgical procedure, a female kitten is also likely to be up and about almost immediately, seemingly none the worse for the experience. She may be drowsy for a few hours because of the anaesthetic, but should be back to normal by the next morning. Some cats try to remove their stitches, so keep a close eye on your kitten. If you have any worries at all, contact your vet for advice.

Will neutering affect your kitten's weight?

All neutered animals have a tendency to lay down surplus fat, and could put on a little weight. This occurs partly because their priorities change – they expend less energy out and about, patrolling territory (in the case of a tom) and looking for mates, and activities such as eating become more interesting.

However, cats are very good at limiting their food intake to suit their needs, and, provided that you check regularly that your kitten is not becoming fat, there should be no problem. In any event, the risks of putting on weight are certainly less significant than those of an entire tom's lifestyle, the risks of pregnancy and birth for a female and, of course, the possibility of unwanted kittens.

Dark fur patches

In some female cats, such as the Siamese, the fur which grows back over the operation site can be much darker than on the rest of the body. This is because the exposed area of skin will be at a lower temperature – as are the colour points of a Siamese (see page 26) – making the fur grow back darker.

Neutered cats tend to gain surplus fat, so weigh your cat regularly, as shown (remember to deduct the weight of the carrier), and keep a record. If you are concerned about your cat's weight, talk to your vet.

This darker fur will eventually grow out as the kitten loses and regrows hair naturally. However, if you intend to show your kitten in neuter classes and wish to avoid a dark patch, bandage a piece of padding over the operation site and keep the cat in a heated room (approximately 24°C, or 75°F) until the hair has re-grown.

THE MATURE CAT

Your cat will reach its full physical size by the time it is 12–18 months old (depending on its breed or type, and on other health factors). Its coat may develop further and the colour may change a little, depending again on its breed or type. The cat will also have passed the most hazardous period of its life, when accidents were most likely to happen, and, having got this far, is likely to be with you for many years to come.

It is a good idea to weigh your cat regularly at this point. Up until now, it is unlikely to have put on excessive fat because it has been growing rapidly, but growth will now stop and the cat will be at its mature weight. Keeping a record of this will help you to calculate later on whether it has put on too much weight or has lost weight for any reason, and to take the appropriate action.

The way your cat looks at this age will change very little for at least the next 10 years, if not more. The rate of ageing and the way in which individuals show their age vary from cat to cat, and also to some extent from breed to breed.

On average cats now live to about 14 years of age, thanks to better nutrition, preventive vaccinations and health care, and good veterinary care. However, many can and do go on to their late teens, or even longer. Siamese and Burmese cats are said to be fairly long-lived and regularly reach their late teens, although – just like humans – some look ancient by the age of nine (the human equivalent of 50) while others look positively youthful at 16 (the human equivalent of 80).

It is very difficult to age a mature cat accurately, which could be anything from three to 13 years old and yet still look fit and move with agility and speed. Most 20-year-old cats do tend to look a little unkempt, but in general cats age very gracefully, and much more so than their canine counterparts.

CARE INTO OLD AGE

As the years go by your older cat may begin to suffer the ravages of time, but some fairly simple actions on your part should ensure that its life remains carefree and comfortable.

Your cat will reach physical maturity between 12 and 18 months of age; at this stage it will be the equivalent of a 15-year-old person.

Regular veterinary check-ups

While 'old age' is not in itself a disease, it does cause the body's systems to become less efficient in a number of ways. This means that, while in its youth a cat may have suffered from one disease at a time, as an older cat it is likely to be troubled by a combination of problems which may interact with one another.

155

The key to good health care for your older cat lies in vigilance. Take your cat to the vet for a thorough physical check-up twice a year (rather than just once a year when vaccination boosters were due, as you did when it was younger), so that the vet can pick up any signs of kidney, heart, or other problems as early as possible. You may like to begin these check-ups when your cat reaches the age of nine or 10. If there is nothing wrong, your mind will be set at rest; if a problem does arise, early treatment will be much more effective.

Some vets now even run special clinics for older pets, recognizing the need for spending a little extra time on these much-cherished companions and dealing with any problems quickly.

Monitoring your cat at home

Regular veterinary check-ups are very important in later years, but you should also keep a watchful eye on your older cat on a day-to-day basis. Continue with your own regular health checks, and take note of the cat's general well-being. If you monitor the basics and notice anything unusual – for example, if your cat is not eating well, is drinking water excessively, or seems to have trouble passing urine or faeces – you can report these observations to your vet so that he or she can investigate the cause and treat it as necessary. Veterinary medicine is continually advancing, and a great deal can now be done to help, so never write off an aged cat too early.

Your cat's environment

Look afresh at your cat's environment as the years roll on. Does the cat have difficulty in making the leap up to its favourite perch on the windowsill, and does the jump down seem to jolt its whole body? If so, make things easier with a re-positioned chair or stool, so that the steps up are smaller and the descent more gentle.

Similarly, is that stiff old cat flap proving a struggle to operate or snapping shut on your cat's tail, or is the step on either side too high? Is the cat feeling the cold a little more because it is less active, and because its coat is not quite so oily and well kept? Perhaps a bed on or near a radiator, or a hot-water bottle wrapped in a towel on very cold nights, will provide additional comfort.

Your cat may also appreciate a gentle wipe with dampened cotton wool or a soft cloth and warm water to clean any discharge from the eyes. A long-haired cat may need extra attention to keep its coat free from mats, especially under the tail.

Keep an eye on claws, too, which may become overgrown. Older cats also seem less able to retract their more brittle claws as fully as when they were young, perhaps because the elasticity of the muscles and tendons holding them in place has decreased. As a result, the claws tend to remain slightly unsheathed and may catch in upholstery or carpets, causing pain and distress.

Changes in behaviour

Your cat's behaviour may alter with age. While most cats sleep more and generally get on with life without causing a fuss, some seem to feel more vulnerable, and demand reassurance and attention. Some of the more vocal breeds such as the Siamese or Burmese can become very chatty, and will certainly let you know when they need something – be it food or a cuddle, or simply to find out where you are in the house.

The need for reassurance can often manifest itself in 'night calling', where a cat waits until the house is quiet and everyone is cosily asleep, and then cries as if on its last legs. As soon as its panicking owner appears and shows concern, the cat yawns deeply and drops off to sleep, reassured that it has not been abandoned. If your cat shows a need for security in its later years, you could perhaps move its bed into your bedroom, provide a radio for company, or even set up a baby intercom so that you can voice reassurance without having to get out of bed on each occasion. Otherwise, make sure that the area in which the cat sleeps is warm and cosy, and try to be patient – it is a small price to pay for many years of love and companionship.

As your cat grows older, taking it for regular physical check-ups is even more important, so that your vet can detect any signs of ill-health at an early stage. Older individuals can tend to put on too much weight – as this 10-year-old cat has done – so continue to weigh your cat regularly, and adjust its food intake as necessary.

USEFUL ADDRESSES

Association of Pet Behaviour Counsellors (APBC)
PO Box 46, Worcester WR8 9YS
Tel: 01386-751151

Cats' Protection League
17 King's Road, Horsham,
West Sussex RH13 5PN
Tel: 01403-221900

Feline Advisory Bureau (FAB)
Taeselbury, High Street, Tisbury,
Wiltshire SP3 6LZ
Tel: 01747-871872
(Information sheets on many feline diseases available)

FAB Boarding-cattery Information Service
1 Church Close, Orcheston,
Salisbury, Wiltshire SP3 4RP
Tel: 01980-620251
(A list of FAB-approved boarding catteries is available for £2; this also contains a 10-point guide of what to look for and how to assess what you see when you visit a cattery)

Governing Council of the Cat Fancy (GCCF)
4–6 Penel Orlieu, Bridgwater,
Somerset TA6 3PG
Tel: 01278-427575

Royal Society for the Prevention of Cruelty to Animals (RSPCA)
Couseway, Horsham,
West Sussex RH12 1HG
Tel: 01403-264181

FURTHER READING

Books
Do Cats Need Shrinks? Peter Neville
(Sidgwick & Jackson, third edition 1990)

How to Talk to Your Cat Claire Bessant
(Smith Gryphon Ltd, 1992)

The Cat's Mind Bruce Fogle
(Pelham Books, 1991)

The Complete Guide to Kitten Care
Mark Evans
(Mitchell Beazley, 1996)

The Manual of Feline Behaviour
Valerie O'Farrell and Peter Neville
(Blackwell Science Ltd, 1994)

The True Nature of the Cat
John Bradshaw
(Boxtree Ltd, 1993)

The Ultrafit Older Cat Claire Bessant,
Peter Neville and Bradley Viner
(Smith Gryphon Ltd, 1993)

Magazines
All About Cats
Gong Publishing Group (Suite C),
21 Heathlands Road,
London SW6 4GP
Tel: 0171-384 3261

Cats
5 James Leigh Street,
Manchester M1 5NF
Tel: 0161-236 0577

Your Cat
Apex House, Oundle Road,
Peterborough,
Cambridgeshire PE2 9NP
Tel: 01733-898100

PICTURE CREDITS

INDEX